WITHDRAWN

Realistic Wildlife Painting *for* DECORATIVE ARTISTS

Realistic Wildlife Painting
for DECORATIVE ARTISTS

Heather Dakota

NORTH LIGHT BOOKS
CINCINNATI, OHIO
www.nlbooks.com

About the Author

Heather Dakota has been painting for twenty years. She has a Bachelor of Fine Arts degree from the University of Central Florida and for the last several years has been teaching decorative painting at local retail shops, and regional and national decorative painting conventions. Heather started creating her own designs based on her love of nature, especially wildlife. She has received many awards for her creations, including several first-place awards and most recently a third-place award at the Heart of Ohio Tole Convention art show in Columbus. Heather lives in the Midwest where she raises her sons, tends her garden and continues her closeness to, and appreciation of, the earth and its riches.

PHOTO BY DEBORAH GALLOWAY

Realistic Wildlife Painting for Decorative Artists. Copyright © 2000 by Heather Dakota. Manufactured in China. All rights reserved. The patterns and drawings in this book are for the personal use of the decorative painter. By permission of the author and publisher, they may be either hand-traced or photocopied to make single copies, but under no circumstances may they be resold or republished. It is permissible for the purchaser to paint the designs contained herein and sell them at fairs, bazaars and craft shows. No other part of this book may be reproduced in any form or by any electronic or mechanical means including information storage and retrieval systems without permission in writing from the publisher, except by a reviewer, who may quote brief passages in a review. Published by North Light Books, an imprint of F&W Publications, Inc., 1507 Dana Avenue, Cincinnati, Ohio 45207. (800) 289-0963. First edition.

Other fine North Light Books are available from your local bookstore, art supply store or direct from the publisher.

04 03 02 01 00   5 4 3 2 1

Library of Congress Cataloging-in-Publication Data

Dakota, Heather
  Realistic wildlife painting for decorative artists / Heather Dakota.
    p. cm.
  Includes index.
  ISBN 1-58180-013-4 (alk. paper)-- ISBN 0-89134-939-1 (pbk. alk. paper)
    1. Wildlife painting--Technique. I. Title.

ND1380 .D35 2000
751.45'432--dc21
                     99-050231

Editor: Christine Doyle
Designer: Brian Roeth
Photographers: Christine Polomsky and Al Parrish
Bird photo on page 9 courtesy of Diane Knerr

Dedication

I would like to dedicate this book to my sons, Jacob and Jeremiah, who constantly inspire me and help me keep a childlike curiosity about everything.

Acknowledgments

I would like to thank my family and friends for their constant support and encouragement. Mom, this book would not be possible without you. To Dad and Joyce, thank you for oohing and ahing over even my not-so-good paintings. Carrie, you're my best friend, and you always have gum. What more can a sister ask for, except a brother-in-law like Skip who puts up with all my phone calls. Joe, thank you for your energy and spirit. It has kept me going more times than I can count. To my Father, thank you for my creative life. To Wendy, you are a tried-and-true friend, so what's the next adventure? For my love of nature and wildlife, I must thank Grandpa Al.

I would also like to thank Rosemary Reynolds at DecoArt for supplying me with wonderful paint. For offering some fantastic surfaces for my creative juices, a big thank-you to Jeff Foster at Cabin Crafters, Heather Redick, Crews Country Pleasures, Woodcrafts and S & G.

Last, but certainly not least, I must thank all the wonderful teachers who have inspired me over the years, especially those in the Art Department at the University of Central Florida and more recently Deanne Fortnam, Peggy Harris, Sherry C. Nelson and Kerry Trout.

A very special thank-you to my editor Christine Doyle, and a wonderful photographer, Christine Polomsky. Thank you for making my thoughts and artwork look great. And to all my associates at F&W Publications, thank you for your support!

TABLE OF CONTENTS

PROJECT ONE

PROJECT TWO

PROJECT THREE

PROJECT FOUR

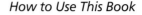

From learning to ride horses with my grandfather to being surrounded by wildlife living in the mountains of Taos, New Mexico, I have developed a keen sense of nature's importance in my life. Nature, wildlife in particular, always seems fresh and exciting. I'm still enchanted by the little black-capped chickadee that visits my bird feeder, and the raccoon that likes to sleep in my tree. Even the squirrels that haven't learned they can't get to the bird feeders and the wonderful mammals and birds I've seen on my many hikes into the wilderness fascinate me.

You'll find the most enjoyable part of wildlife painting, aside from the painting itself, is the research involved before you paint. I guess I still have a childlike curiosity about the wild animals I paint, and they continually teach and inspire me. I hope this book will impart to you some of my enthusiasm for painting these magnificent creatures, big and small.

There are several things to remember when painting. First, my techniques can be applied to any animal you want to paint. Second, as many creatures as there are in the world, there are at least that many techniques to paint them. Every wildlife artist will tell you a different way to paint. Your painting may not turn out exactly like mine. That's great! You are an individual artist with your own style of painting. I encourage you to explore and discover that style and continue using it, even while you're working with my designs.

I recommend that all decorative painting enthusiasts join the Society of Decorative Painters. The society offers numerous opportunities for expanding your painting knowledge and creating wonderful fellowships with other decorative painters. For more information, see Resources on page 126.

My hopes in doing this book are to increase your interest in the art world and increase your awareness of the world of abundant wildlife around us. A portion of the proceeds from this book will be used to protect the endangered species of North America and the world, through Save the Manatee, Raptor, Inc. and Friends of the Forest sponsorship programs.

Best of luck with your creative endeavors!

Heather

How to Use This Book

The wildlife designs in this book were created with the idea that you can copy them to develop your painting skills. Here is a clarification of what you are allowed to do with the designs. First, you may enlarge or reduce them by hand or take them to a copy center and have them mechanically enlarged. Under copyright law, you do need written permission to do so. Consider this written permission. You may need to show this passage to the copy center.

Also, you may enter your paintings in shows and use these designs to teach other students. If you duplicate one of my paintings, you may sell your work with your name on it. However, it would be unfair to mislead clients into believing that you were the original artist. Therefore, under your signature, put that the original artist was Heather Dakota.

It is my sincerest hope that you will learn from my designs. Combine them with your style, and begin to develop your own originals.

CHAPTER ONE

Getting Started

Gathering Reference Material

A reference file is very important in painting wildlife. There are many different kinds of reference materials. We'll talk about a few here.

Photographs

Photos give you a chance to plan your painting, and they provide some of the best reference materials. Not only can you take pictures of the animals, but you can take pictures of their habitats, especially the flowers and trees that grow nearby. You can add interest to your painting using photographs of old junk—watering cans and garden tools, horse equipment and fences.

There are several good places to take photographs of wildlife. The best place is in the wild, but sometimes this is not an option. So, the next best place would be a zoo. I'm lucky. I live very close to the Cincinnati Zoo, one of the best in the country. The problem with taking photographs of zoo animals is they don't behave as they would in the wild. Simply keep this in mind. Another good place to take photos is your own backyard. If you're lucky enough to have wilderness in your backyard, you'll have an abundance of reference photographs. If you live in the city, you'll find it a little more difficult, but not impossible. If you hang bird feeders and other wildlife attractors, you'll be surprised at the wildlife that

comes to visit you.

If photography is not one of your special talents, keep in mind that photos don't need to be perfect, just in focus. If it would make you feel more comfortable, you may want to take a basic course in photography. Even a photograph of an animal that is far away can lend itself to your painting. Remember, too, you can mix and match photographs to come up with a pleasing composition. If you do use two or more photographs, make sure the light is coming from the same direction.

Tips for Putting Together Reference Material

- When taking photographs of wildlife, start with good camera equipment. You can take photos at the zoo or at state and national parks.
- Keep a sketchbook with you at all times. You never know when an opportunity will present itself.
- Make a photo file of things that interest you. You might need them for reference on a future project.
- Organize your reference material. If the material is in order, you'll find it much easier to be inspired.

The most helpful tool in reference photography is, of course, a camera. Even a simple point-and-shoot will give you a decent reference photograph. If you plan to do a lot of wildlife painting, it might be a good idea for you to invest in a good camera. I have two cameras: a Canon EOS with a macro lens and a Pentax K1000 with a standard 50mm lens. The Canon EOS allows me to take close-ups that show a lot of details. The macro lens allows me to get a close-up photograph of an animal I would rather not get near, such as the white bengal tiger.

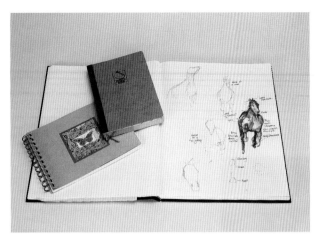

A sketchbook is one of the handiest tools to have when gathering reference materials.

While the pictures in the books are copyrighted, they are great references for color and anatomical accuracy.

Sketchbook

For all the fancy equipment, there is nothing better than your own observation. I strongly recommend you carry a sketchbook with you everywhere. I recently found myself only ten feet from a beautiful Cooper's hawk. But I didn't have my camera or sketchbook, so I missed an opportunity to capture some great reference material.

If you feel sketching is not one of your strengths, remember that practice will improve your drawing skills and no one else has to see what you've drawn. It's simply for you. Additionally, a sketchbook will allow you to record the weather and your feelings. When you begin to paint your animals, these will be very important. When you're using a sketchbook, a pair of binoculars is another good tool to have handy. Like the macro lens, they will bring you in close to pick up on subtle details and keep you at a safe distance so you don't get hurt or disturb the animal.

Books and Magazines

If getting out in the wilderness to get a photograph of your favorite wild animal is out of the question, then books and magazines are the next best thing to being there. Remember, however, that the photos are copyrighted. Be careful how you use the photographs you find in books and magazines. They also make excellent supplemental reference material to your own photographs.

Wildlife Videos and TV Shows

I've found wildlife videos and television shows to be excellent sources of reference material. They show wildlife in their natural habitats, doing what they do in the wild. If you see a scene or animal position that you think would make an interesting painting, you can just stop the video. National Geographics has some of the best videos.

Several shows on Public Television, including *Nature*, *National Geographic Explorer* and *Kratts' Creatures*, will help you pick up on animal details, habitat and behavior. Another fabulous wildlife show is *Wild America*, which explores the animal's habitat and behavior and often shows the animals close up so you can see the fine details.

Videos are a wonderful source for witnessing wildlife in its natural habitat.

How to Enlarge Your Design

There are several methods of enlarging a design to fit a larger surface, such as a piece of furniture. Perhaps one of these will work for you.

Slide Enlargement

My favorite method of enlargement is to take a reference slide and project the image onto the wall or, if the projector is mounted on a copy stand, onto the table. This is a great way to make a very accurate line drawing, and you don't have to worry about your drawing skills. The only disadvantages to this method is your arm will get tired if you're making your drawing on the wall, and the room must be dark enough for you to see the projection.

Opaque Projector

Another one of my favorite methods of enlargement is using an opaque projector. It works in much the same way as a slide projector, but with this device you can enlarge the actual drawing or reference photograph, and some even reduce the image. The original drawing can be done on almost any type of paper that will fit into the projector. You can then trace the reference to your transfer paper or acetate. However, I've found that the enlargement size is somewhat limited. If you want an oversized enlargement for a large piece of furniture or a wall, you need to move the projector to different parts of the original drawing, and it must be done in the dark. I find these minor inconveniences.

Preparing Your Surface

If you are going to paint on an already finished piece of furniture, you'll first need to cover its original finish. If you're unsure what to do, there are several good books on this subject or you can ask at your local home improvement store. I use Kilz to cover the original finish. First sand the original finish. Then, brush on Kilz to cover. You may need two coats.

If you are painting on unfinished wood, you'll need to fill all the nail holes, cracks and wood knots. I use J.W. etc. Professional Wood Filler. Let the wood filler dry. Once the irregularities are filled and dry, sand the entire piece. While you're sanding, make sure you use a dust mask to protect your lungs from the dust particles. You may want to wear goggles to keep the wood dust out of your eyes. After sanding your piece, wipe the dust off with a tack cloth. You are now ready to seal the wood.

I use J.W. etc. First-Step Wood Sealer. You can also mix this with your basecoat color to seal the wood and apply the basecoat at the same time. Be sure you read the instructions on the bottle.

Now you're ready to transfer your pattern. Make a copy of the pattern, and tape it to your surface with masking tape on only one edge of the pattern. Slide a piece of graphite paper underneath (use dark graphite paper for light basecoats and white for dark basecoats). Trace the pattern with a stylus, using enough pressure to transer a clear pattern without denting a wooden surface.

Photocopier

I'm sure many of you have used a photocopier to enlarge a design from a project book. I use photocopiers to enlarge or even reduce my own designs. You'll find they offer a wide range of sizes for very little money.

Computer

There are several computer programs, such as QuarkXPress and Adobe Photoshop, that will take a scanned piece of artwork and enlarge or reduce the image. Then, you can print the image in several sections to have a large completed transfer. This method is fairly expensive if you need to purchase the programs.

Materials

The designs in this book can be transferred to any number of surfaces, including terra-cotta, wood, tin and porcelain.

The brushes used for these projects include liners, rounds, filberts, flats, rakes and scruffy brushes.

Caring For and Cleaning Your Brushes

Brushes are an expensive investment. To help them last a long time, here are some hints for you.

- Never let paint dry in your brushes.
- Do not scrape your brushes on the bottom of the brush basin. Tap them against the sides to remove paint.
- Clean your brushes after each painting session with J.W. etc. Formula II Creme Brush Cleaner. Follow the directions on the bottle.
- Do not let your brushes dry standing on their handles. Dry the handles and ferrules, then lightly dry the bristles after cleaning. The best way to let the bristles dry is to hang the brushes ferrules down. If this isn't possible, allow them to dry lying flat.
- Make sure you reshape the brushes after each cleaning.
- Never let brushes stand in water. This will bend the bristles out of shape.

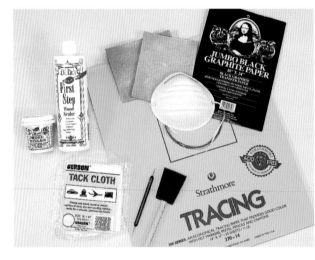

These are the supplies you'll need to prepare your wooden surface for painting.

Surfaces

There are so many surfaces to choose from—wood, slate, tin, terra-cotta, porcelain, glass and walls. You can use any surface that will fit your needs. Any of my designs can be enlarged or reduced to fit the surface you want to use. I prefer using wood.

Preparation Materials

Preparing your surface for painting is a very important step and should not be rushed. You'll need different grades of sand paper or pads, a dust mask, goggles, a tack cloth, J.W. etc. Professional Wood Filler, J.W. etc. First-Step Wood Sealer, a sponge brush, tracing paper and graphite paper.

Brushes

I do not have a particular brand of brush that I think is better than another. You'll need an assortment of liners, rounds, flats, rakes and scruffy brushes in a variety of sizes. The rake brush is a must for painting realistic fur. In each project, I indicate which type of brush I'm using, but I want you to use the brush you feel comfortable painting with. The size of the brush you use should depend on the size of your chosen surface. However, this is not a hard-and-fast rule. You can use a small brush on a large surface. It just may take you a little longer to complete the painting.

Gather all of your supplies before you start painting, and place them in the same spot each time you paint.

Acrylic paints today come in so many wonderful colors. While DecoArt Americana paints are used in these projects, feel free to substitute your favorite brand.

General Supplies

Here are the things that will help you in your painting. You can use all of these or just the items that suit your needs. I use a drop cloth for all of my pieces, especially the large furniture pieces. Also, because I work with acrylics, which dry very quickly, I use a wet palette. However, I use paper towels in the palette instead of a sponge and the palette paper. I place my paints directly on the paper towel. This keeps my paints workable for a long time. After each use, during my painting session or whenever my paints are developing a skin, I give them a mist of clean water. I also make sure the lid is on the wet palette very tight when I'm finished painting. Some other supplies that help are a blow-dryer, sponges, palette knife, brush basin, stylus, pencil and kneaded eraser.

Paint

I use DecoArt Americana paint. I find that it gives wonderful coverage, and the color selection is fantastic. Feel free to use your favorite brand of paint. I prefer using acrylics because of their low impact on the enviroment and their speedy drying time. My techniques will work with oils as well. You can

Taking the time to finish your project properly will protect your painting and give your piece a professional look.

match the colors with the color charts provided with each project.

Finishing

Finishing your project will give it a professional quality that everyone will admire.

First, remove any graphite lines that are still showing. I use a kneaded eraser. Varnish your project with several coats of J.W. etc. Right-Step Varnish. You decide whether you want a matte, satin or glossy finish. Make sure that each coat dries before you apply the next coat. After your third coat has dried, dip your pink sanding pad in a cup of water with a drop of dish soap. Rub the damp pad on the surface in a circu-

lar motion, pressing lightly. Your surface will turn dull, but don't worry. Dry it with a paper towel. Apply the next coat of varnish, let dry, then sand again with soapy sanding pad. Repeat after each subsequent coat of varnish. For a truly professional look to your project, apply a total of eight coats of varnish, though I've heard of other painters who have applied up to twenty-five. Let your final coat dry overnight, then buff it with very fine steel wool, until you have a smooth matte finish. Be sure to wear a dust mask when using the steel wool. If you desire, buff the surface with a finishing wax and cheesecloth.

CHAPTER TWO

Terms and Techniques

Basecoating

Basecoating is painting your entire surface with one color that serves as the base color. You will need to apply at least two coats to achieve complete and even coverage. Basecoating also refers to filling in or undercoating parts of your design area. Always apply your basecoat smoothly and evenly.

Sideloading a Brush

STEP 1: Wet your brush and blot it on a paper towel.

STEP 2: Dip one corner of the brush into the paint.

STEP 3: Stroke the brush on your waxed palette first on one side of the brush and then the other. This will fully load your brush with paint.

STEP 4: A properly sideloaded brush will have a soft blend of color from the loaded corner that fades to water on the opposite corner. Use a sideloaded brush to float color (see page 15).

Back-to-Back Float

To create a soft blend of color in the middle of an area, dampen the surface with water. Then, with a sideloaded brush, float the color down one side of the area, then turn the brush over and float the color down the other side. Overlap and soften the float edges where they join.

Circle Float

To create a soft circular highlight, first lightly dampen the surface with water. (Make sure it's not too wet.) Place the loaded corner of a side-loaded brush in the middle of the highlight area and pat the brush around the center point, always with the loaded corner of the brush toward the center point.

Hard-Edged Float

For a hard-edged float, sideload the brush as above, but do not dampen the surface. Start at one side and float the color along the edge of the area and over to the other side. You will use this technique when painting wildlife eyes.

Stippling

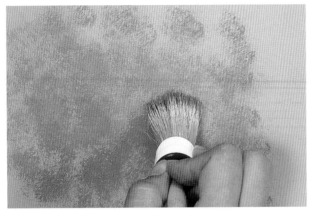

Stippling is done by taking a loaded dry brush and pouncing the color lightly on your surface. This works well to create background grass and foliage.

Drybrushing

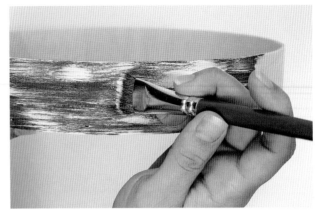

Painting with a dry brush results in wispy color, as opposed to the solid color achieved with a wet brush. Load the dry brush lightly with paint, tap it out on a paper towel and brush the surface.

Sponging

STEP 1: Sponging creates a mottled effect. First load a sea sponge or regular household sponge with paint and rub it on your waxed palette to remove the excess paint.

STEP 2: Pounce it on your surface in a random pattern.

STEP 3: To soften the sponging, use a mop brush to blend any too-harsh sponge marks.

Spattering

Spattering is creating tiny drops of paint by using a toothbrush or a spattering tool. The paint needs to be thinned with water to achieve this look. The thinner the paint, the larger the drops. Load thinned paint on an old toothbrush and run your finger over the bristles, allowing the paint to hit your surface.

Antiquing

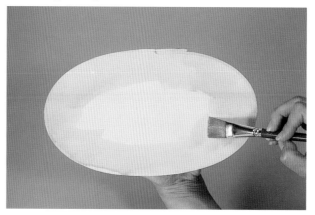

Antiquing is a technique that can be used to give your surface an aged look. Wipe on a thin layer of oil paint, or wall glaze mixed with acrylic paint (usually brown or black), before or after painting. Then, wipe off the excess, especially toward the inside surface area.

Crackling

Crackling is another technique used to give your piece an aged look. Basecoat your surface and allow to dry. Apply the crackle medium according to the package directions, then paint over the dried crackle medium with a topcoat.

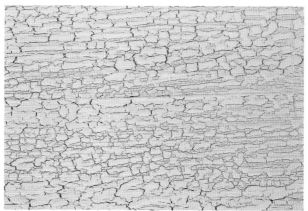

The finished effect is of aged, cracked paint.

❧ HINT ❧ *When you paint over the dried crackle medium, do not go back over your strokes. The paint will smear and lose the crackled look.*

Rag Scrubbing

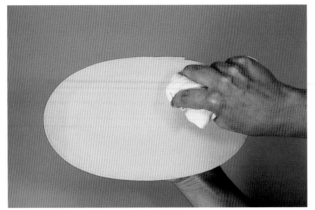

Rag scrubbing creates a soft antique effect. Basecoat your surface and allow to dry. Mix glazing medium with your chosen color (I often use a slightly darker value of the basecoat color). Paint small areas with this mix. Using a rag (a clean cloth diaper works great), rub the paint into the basecoat, but do not rub it off.

Color Washing

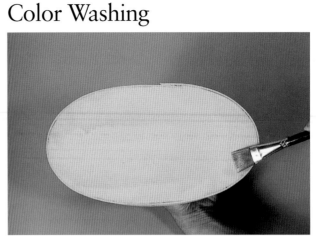

For a color wash, thin the paint with enough water so that you can still see the basecoat when the wash is applied to the surface.

Scumbling

Scumbling is a process of blending colors that produces a mottled effect. I used this technique to create the background for the chipmunk project.

STEP 1: Apply the basecoat. While the color is still wet, pick up a second color on your dirty brush and begin making choppy strokes moving toward the center. If you need more paint, pick up more of one of the colors.

STEP 2: You can add several other colors in the same manner. Blend each color away from where you began to apply it.

Painting Fur

STEP 1: For the most realistic fur, begin working generally, in large areas, and move to more detailed work in small areas. Use a flat brush to undercoat the large areas.

STEP 2: As you refine the fur, begin using a rake brush. Hold the brush at a 45° angle to the surface, making short strokes in the direction of the fur growth.

STEP 3: To refine fur even more, lightly touch the very tip of the bristles to the surface and make wispy strokes, creating individual hairs.

STEP 4: You can also use the rake brush in a vertical position for longer fur.

STEP 5: You can use the flat of the brush for shorter fur. Or to refine the fur even more, put in random hairs with a liner brush using the shading and highlighting colors. It is very effective to put a few darker hairs in the highlight areas and a few lighter hairs in the shading areas.

Color Choices for Painting Fur

White Fur

White fur has a base color of off-white (in this case Light Buttermilk) with Titanium White highlights. The shading color is a Burnt Umber or Lamp Black. You can make a variety of shades by mixing any of these colors together.

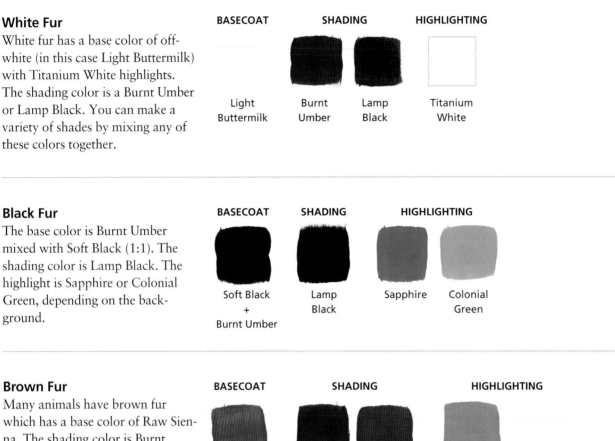

BASECOAT	SHADING		HIGHLIGHTING
Light Buttermilk	Burnt Umber	Lamp Black	Titanium White

Black Fur

The base color is Burnt Umber mixed with Soft Black (1:1). The shading color is Lamp Black. The highlight is Sapphire or Colonial Green, depending on the background.

BASECOAT	SHADING	HIGHLIGHTING	
Soft Black + Burnt Umber	Lamp Black	Sapphire	Colonial Green

Brown Fur

Many animals have brown fur which has a base color of Raw Sienna. The shading color is Burnt Umber or Burnt Sienna. It is highlighted with Mink Tan and Light Buttermilk. A variety of shades can be made by mixing any of these five colors.

BASECOAT	SHADING		HIGHLIGHTING	
Raw Sienna	Burnt Umber	Burnt Sienna	Mink Tan	Light Buttermilk

Orange Fur

Orange fur is painted with light, medium and dark shades of orange. You can mix the orange with white or black for the highlighting and shading colors. In this case, I didn't mix the colors. I used Georgia Clay for the base color. The shading color is Burnt Sienna or Burnt Umber, and the highlighting colors are Cadmium Orange, Pumpkin and Tangerine.

BASECOAT	SHADING		HIGHLIGHTING		
Georgia Clay	Burnt Sienna	Burnt Umber	Cadmium Orange	Pumpkin	Tangerine

Painting Animal Eyes

While the size, shape and color of eyes varies among types of animals, the method of painting is much the same.

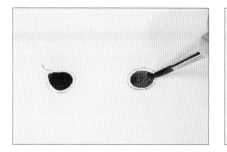

STEP 1: Basecoat the iris and pupil.

STEP 2: Outline the eye.

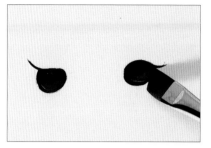

STEP 3: Shade the top half of the eye with a hard-edged float (see page 15) of the eye shading color side-loaded on a flat brush. This is the shadow cast by the eyelid.

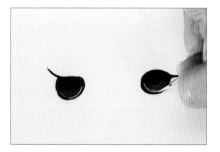

STEP 4: If the light source is on the left-hand side, paint the reflective light on the bottom right of the eyeball. It is just a thin line with the eye highlight color.

STEP 5: Paint another darker highlight on the bottom left side of the eyeball. This highlight meets the lighter highlight.

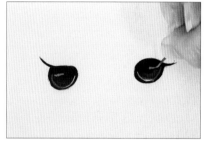

STEP 6: With a liner brush loaded with the basecoat color, paint the reflection of the sky. Dab the brush, making a thin and bumpy line. For this eye, I made the line ⅛-inch wide by ¼-inch long, but the line should be wider and longer if the eye is larger.

STEP 7: Lastly, add the reflection of the sun, using a liner brush tipped in white. Apply this highlight to the left eye at ten o'clock and the right eye at two o'clock. If the right eye is in heavy shadow, do not apply the highlight or apply it with white mixed with the basecoat color.

Chipmunk in the Strawberry Patch

Not long ago, I lived on a small farm in northern Kentucky. We had a fantastic strawberry patch that would yield a pint of strawberries each night throughout May. The most frustrating thing about having this strawberry patch was the little chipmunks that loved the strawberries as much as my family did. It wasn't a hard thing for me to share my strawberries, but it was difficult for me to see a group of very plump, ripe berries with one nibble out of each of them. Couldn't they just take the whole berry? I caught a culprit one morning munching on a portion of a berry. He took one look at me, stood up on his hind legs and gave a little chipmunk shout. He was obviously angry that I had interrupted his breakfast. Now that's a fine how-do-you-do!

Materials List

SUPPLIES:
preparation supplies
   (see page 12)
general supplies
   (see page 13)
finishing supplies
   (see page 13)
chalk pencil
straightedge
J.W. etc. Exterior Varnish

BRUSHES:
no. 0 liner
no. 4 round
no. 4, no. 6, no. 8 filberts
¼-inch rake
1-inch flat

SURFACE:
16-inch wind chime from
   S & G Products, Inc.

DecoArt Americana Acrylic Paints

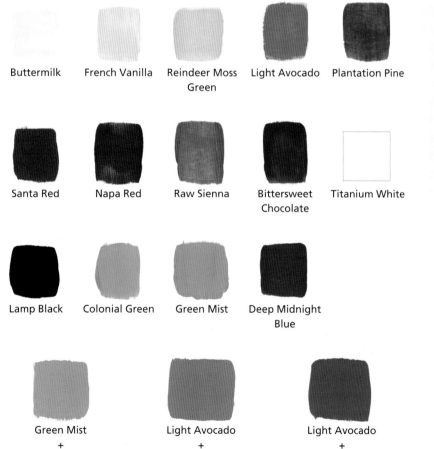

Buttermilk   French Vanilla   Reindeer Moss Green   Light Avocado   Plantation Pine

Santa Red   Napa Red   Raw Sienna   Bittersweet Chocolate   Titanium White

Lamp Black   Colonial Green   Green Mist   Deep Midnight Blue

Green Mist
+
Reindeer Moss Green (1:1)

Light Avocado
+
Colonial Green (3:2)

Light Avocado
+
Deep Midnight Blue (3:1)

Patterns

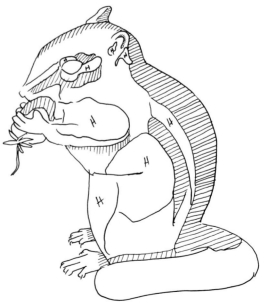

Shading and Highlighting Placement Guide

These patterns may be hand-traced or photocopied for personal use only. Enlarge at 135 percent to bring to size for this project.

Paint the Background

Using a 1-inch flat brush, basecoat all sides of the surface with Buttermilk. When the paint has dried, dampen the surface with clean water and basecoat again with Buttermilk thinned with water. While this is still wet, load a no. 6 filbert or no. 6 flat brush with Plantation Pine and use the scumbling method (see page 18) to blend the colors into the wet background, working in a slip-slap method from the bottom right toward the upper left corner in a *U* shape. You will need to reinforce the darker color several times. Make sure you continue to pick up a little more water on your brush as you go. Always start from the bottom and blend toward the top. When you feel the piece is dark enough, wipe the brush, pick up Buttermilk thinned with water and blend toward the interior of your *U*. As a final touch, randomly blend a tiny bit of Napa Red thinned with water into the wet background.

Basecoat the Chipmunk

Apply the basic outline of the chipmunk using your graphite paper and a stylus. With Raw Sienna on a no. 6 filbert, basecoat the chipmunk body and the centers of his hands and feet. Basecoat his hands with French Vanilla. Apply the pattern details of the chipmunk.

Shade and Highlight the Chipmunk

Sideload a no. 8 filbert with Bitter-sweet Chocolate, and shade the chipmunk. Shade down his back, under his arm, around the top of his head and a little on his lower jaw. Also, base in the darker stripes on his back with a ¼-inch rake brush.

To paint highlights, sideload the cleaned no. 8 filbert with Butter-milk. Highlight the chipmunk's arm in a circle float, from the upper jaw back toward his arm, on top and bottom of his eye, on his belly and inside his ear. Add the light center stripe with the ¼-inch rake.

Base the eye with Lamp Black on a no. 6 filbert.

Fur Growth Guide

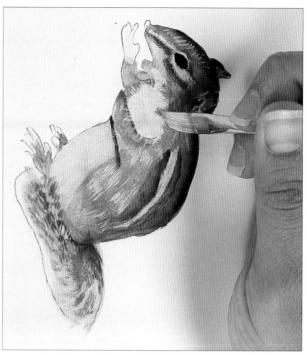

With a damp ¼-inch rake loaded with thinned Bittersweet Chocolate, add fur to the tail, referring to the guide above for fur direction. Add more fur with Lamp Black, French Vanilla and Buttermilk, using this same method and cleaning the brush after each color. Turn your surface, if you wish, so it's more comfortable to paint.

Hold the brush on the vertical and move the brush along the chisel to make long fur. Follow the growth guide and keep in mind the muscles under the fur that would make it ripple and turn.

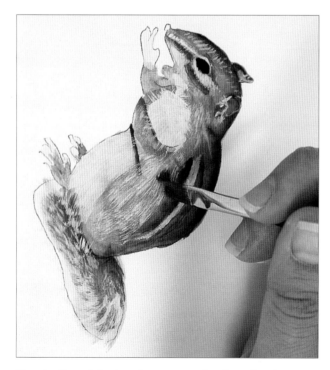

Use the flat of the brush to create the short fur that covers most of the chipmunk body.

For the chipmunk's back, hold the rake brush on the angle, stroking on the chisel. Remember to refer to the growth guide often.

Paint the Strawberry

Basecoat the berry with Reindeer Moss Green. With a no. 6 filbert loaded with Santa Red, shade the berry inside the chipmunk's mouth and around the hand. Add a second shading with a no. 4 filbert side-loaded with Napa Red; cover the same area you did with the first shading. Base the leaves and stem with Light Avocado, and highlight them with Reindeer Moss Green on a no. 0 liner.

Finish the Chipmunk

Base the eye with Lamp Black. Add a highlight of Titanium White at two o'clock with the no. 0 liner brush. Line the bottom of each finger and toe with thinned Raw Sienna. To create the nails, load the liner brush with slightly thinned Lamp Black, lightly touch the brush to the surface and lift to the tip. Curve the nails inward slightly.

⚜ **HINT** ⚜ *If you don't feel comfortable placing the eye highlight with the liner brush, you can use a stylus.*

Basecoat the Strawberries and the Leaves

Basecoat the warm-colored leaves with Light Avocado and the cool (background leaves) with Light Avocado and Colonial Green mix. Basecoat all of the strawberries with Reindeer Moss Green.

Shade the Strawberries

Ripe Berries

Shade the ripe strawberries using a no. 6 filbert brush sideloaded with Santa Red. Shade all around the outside edge of the berry, leaving a highlighted area on the top part of each berry.

Unripe Berries

Shade the unripe berry with a sideload of Light Avocado on a no. 6 filbert, and then again with a no. 4 filbert brush sideloaded with Plantation Pine.

Add a Second Shading

When the shading is finished, crosshatch the berries with a chalk pencil and straightedge. On the unripe berry, place dots of Light Avocado in the center of each diamond with a no. 0 liner. On the ripe berries, place a dot of Santa Red on the highlight areas and dots of Napa Red toward the edges. Erase the crosshatch lines.

Shade the Leaves

First shade the warm leaves with a sideload of Plantation Pine on a no. 6 filbert. Clean the brush, then shade the cool leaves with a sideload mix of Light Avocado and Deep Midnight Blue. Using the same mix sideloaded on the no. 6 filbert, create a back-to-back float (see page 15) down the center of each leaf. Also, shade where the leaves are tucked behind a berry or under another leaf.

Highlight the Strawberries and Leaves

The Strawberries

Flatten a no. 4 round brush and sideload with Reindeer Moss Green. Highlight in the upper right-hand corner of the diamond shape. Increase the highlight with lines of Buttermilk. With Light Avocado loaded on a no. 0 liner, place a seed over the dots.

The Leaves

Highlight the warm leaves using a no. 6 filbert brush sideloaded with Reindeer Moss Green. Highlight the cool leaves with the Green Mist and Reindeer Moss Green mix. With this same mix on the no. 0 liner brush, create an oval float on the left and left sides of the leaves.

⌘ HINT ⌘ *Your light source is coming from the right-hand side. Therefore the opposite side will be shaded.*

Finish the Project

Apply several coats of J.W. etc. Right-Step Satin Varnish, just as you would for a wooden surface. If your wind chime is going outdoors, apply several layers of J.W. etc. Exterior Varnish after the initial coats to protect the wind chime from the weather.

My Little Joey (Koalas)

Koalas are amazing creatures. They are marsupials and carry their young in a pouch. They look cute and cuddly with their soft, thick fur, round ears and large hairless noses, but they are definitely wild animals. Unfortunately, their numbers are on a decline due to habitat destruction. They have specific and specialized habitat requirements that are slowly disappearing. There has been some talk of including the koala on the threatened species list. By painting this project, you can enjoy this adorable animal and express hope for her future.

Materials List

SUPPLIES:
preparation supplies
  (see page 12)
general supplies
  (see page 13)
finishing supplies
  (see page 13)
brown paper bag
extra-fine sanding pad
DecoArt Brush 'n Blend
  Extender

BRUSHES:
no. 2 script liner
no. 6 round
¼-inch rake
no. 10, 1-inch flat
small scruffy

SURFACE:
pegged shelf from
  Cabin Crafters

DecoArt Americana Acrylic Paints

Titanium White	Dove Grey	Slate Grey	Graphite
Charcoal Grey	Burnt Sienna	Hauser Medium Green	Jade Green
Antique Gold	Warm Neutral	Antique Green	Buttermilk
Titanium White + Warm Neutral (3:1)	Dove Grey + Warm Neutral (3:1)	Slate Grey + Warm Neutral (3:1)	Graphite + Warm Neutral (3:1)

Pattern
This pattern may be hand-traced or
photocopied for personal use only.
Enlarge to 116 percent to bring to
size for this project.

*Shading and Highlighting
Placement Guide*

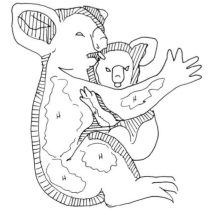

Basecoat the Surface

Using a 1-inch flat brush, spread a layer of Brush 'n Blend medium on the flat surface. Without cleaning your brush, load the same brush with Buttermilk, and beginning in the top left corner, spread the paint diagonally toward the lower right corner. Wipe the brush on a paper towel, but *do not* put it in water. Pick up more of the blending medium and some Burnt Sienna. Starting in the lower right corner, blend diagonally up toward the Buttermilk. Blend the colors. Add more of either color until you are satisfied with the blend. Pick up some Antique Green and add a little here and there, but not too much. If at any time you feel the paint getting sticky, pick up a little more blending medium.

Basecoat the edges and back with Antique Green and any secondary edges, including the pegs, with Antique Gold. Let the surface dry for at least an hour, then sand lightly with a brown paper bag. Apply the pattern with a stylus and graphite paper.

Basecoat the Koalas and Tree

Create approximately a half-dollar size of each of the paint mixes shown on page 35. The Warm Neutral in these mixes adds warmth to the cold, gray colors. Put all the mixes on your wet palette.

Begin by basecoating the koalas with the Slate Grey mix. Paint only the inside part of the ears and leave an area open for the mother's tongue. Basecoat the tree branches with thinned Burnt Sienna. Reapply the pattern details.

Shade the Koalas

To create depth, use a no. 10 flat brush sideloaded with the Graphite mix to shade the top of the heads; the ears; the backs, legs and feet; the mother's jaw and neck; and the top and bottom of the mother's arm. Basecoat the noses and eyes with Charcoal Grey.

Add Fur

Begin adding the fluffy fur by stippling the Dove Grey mix using a small scruffy brush. Stipple on the face, back and legs. Stay away from the shaded areas. Using a ¼-inch rake brush with the same mix, begin putting the fluff in the ears, making long fur strokes.

Continue Adding Fur

Now, with the small scruffy brush, stipple (see page 16) the Titanium White mix over the Dove Grey mix, but let the first highlight show through. With the ¼-inch rake loaded with Graphite mix, add more hair to the ears.

Finish the Koalas and Tree

Add some light stipples of straight Graphite to the fur. With a no. 10 flat brush, float a little Graphite in the deepest shadow areas. With a no. 2 script liner loaded with Charcoal Grey, outline in the deepest shadows.

Highlight each koala's chin with Titanium White with the small scruffy brush. Add more highlights or shadows as needed.

Paint the mother koala's tongue with a brush mix of Burnt Sienna and Titanium White. Load a thin wash of Charcoal Grey on a 1-inch flat, and brush it over the back, head and arms of the koalas. Add more highlights if needed.

Add Titanium White to the center part of the ears facing you, using a ¼-inch rake brush and tiny strokes that push toward the outside of the ear.

With the 1-inch flat brush, shade the inside of the tree with Charcoal Grey, and highlight it with the same mix of Burnt Sienna and Titanium White using the chisel of the flat brush.

Paint the Leaves

Paint the long eucalyptus leaves with a 1-inch flat brush double-loaded with Hauser Medium Green and Jade Green. Start with the brush on the chisel edge. Add pressure to the brush almost to the ferrule; slide the brush, twist and lift back to the chisel, ending at a 90° angle. Occasionally add a little Antique Green and Antique Gold to the Hauser Medium Green side of the brush to give the leaves more interest.

Finish the Project

Let the painting dry completely, then apply varnish as described on page 13.

Cherokee Rose and Cottontail

Different species of cottontail rabbits are found just about everywhere. I've seen a lot of little cottontails on my hikes around Ohio. On one particular occasion, I saw this little Eastern Cottontail hiding among some wild roses. This scene reminded me of my childhood when my mother would read about Brer Rabbit from the Uncle Remus stories. The rabbit stood up on his hind legs, and I could almost hear him say, "Please don't throw me in that briar patch."

Materials List

SUPPLIES:
preparation supplies
(see page 12)
general supplies
(see page 13)
finishing supplies
(see page 13)
DecoArt Weathered Wood
crackling medium
DecoArt Faux Glazing medium
cotton rag

BRUSHES:
no. 0 liner
no. 4, no. 6 filberts
¼-inch rake
no. 6, 1-inch flats

SURFACE:
desk box, scalloped edge
from Cabin Crafters

DecoArt Americana Acrylic Paints

Antique Green   Dried Basil Green   Cool Neutral   Titanium White

Buttermilk   Mississippi Mud   Mink Tan   Toffee

French Grey
Blue   Raw Sienna   Raw Umber   Soft Black

Lamp Black   Antique Gold   Cadmium
Yellow   Deep Burgundy

Antique Green
+
Raw Umber (2:1)   Antique Green
+
Soft Black (2:1)

Patterns

These patterns may be hand-traced or photocopied for personal use only. Enlarge flowers to 128 percent to bring to size for this project. The rabbit appears here at full size.

This pattern may be hand-traced or photocopied for personal use only. Enlarge to 124 percent to bring to size for this project.

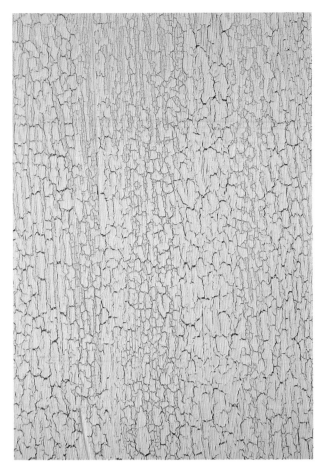

Paint the Background

Basecoat the surface with Deep Burgundy. When this coat is dry (it took mine twenty-four hours), brush on an even coat of Weathered Wood crackling medium with a 1-inch flat brush (see page 17 for more information on crackling). Let this dry for twenty to sixty minutes, then apply a coat of Buttermilk. The effect will be similar to the image at left, which has a basecoat of black and a top coat of Dried Basil Green.

❧ HINT ❧ *When brushing on the Buttermilk, don't go over the same area twice. This will smear the paint and not give you the desired effect.*

When this coat has dried, sand the entire piece with an extra-fine sanding pad, sanding heavily in some areas to remove the paint down to the Deep Burgundy. Now, antique the piece (see page 17) using a 1-inch sponge brush loaded with Antique Green thinned with glazing medium. The antiquing should be darkest along the edges, fading into the center. Use a cotton rag to remove paint from the center, if necessary. You can even spatter some Antique Green glaze mix for a nice aged look. Let dry completely, then apply the basic pattern.

Basecoat the Rabbit

Basecoat the rabbit with Raw Umber. Reapply the pattern details with white graphite and your stylus.

Shading and Highlighting
Placement Guide

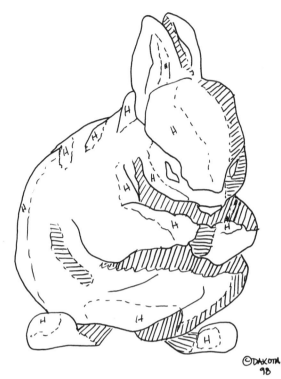

Fur Growth Guide

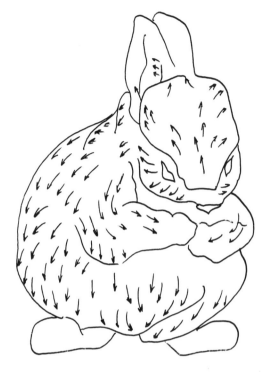

Shade and Highlight the Rabbit

Using Soft Black sideloaded on a no. 6 filbert brush, shade the rabbit in the deepest shadow areas: on the ears, along the eye ridge, under the chin, along the back, under the front paws and arm, and on the feet.

Use Buttermilk loaded on a no. 0 liner brush to paint around the eyes. Basecoat the feet and paws with Buttermilk. Basecoat the eyes with Lamp Black and the nose with Mink Tan. Using a ¼-inch rake brush loaded with Raw Sienna, begin painting the fur, following the fur guide above.

Use the ¼-inch rake loaded with Buttermilk to begin painting the fur on the rabbit's lower belly and lightly around the nose.

Painting the Ears and Hands

STEP 1: Basecoat the ears with Raw Umber, while you basecoat the rest of the rabbit.

STEP 2: Shade the left edge of the left ear with Soft Black using a no. 0 liner brush. Sideload Soft Black on a no. 6 flat brush, and float the shading along the left edge of the right ear. Begin highlighting using the no. 6 flat brush and a brush mix of Toffee and Raw Umber. This mix goes toward the left side of the left ear.

STEP 3: Add Titanium White fur using the ¼-inch rake brush. Paint tufts in the bottom of the left ear going toward the top of the ear. On the right side of the left ear, add little lines on the left side of the ear on the outside of the Soft Black line. Add just a little bit of Titanium White to the right ear toward the middle in a vertical line.

STEP 1: Basecoat the hands with Raw Umber, while you basecoat the rest of the rabbit.

STEP 2: Shade where the hands connect to the body with Soft Black sideloaded on a no. 6 flat brush. Begin highlighting on the tip of the hands with a brush mix of Toffee and Mississippi Mud using the no. 6 flat.

STEP 3: Add the fur first with Buttermilk and then with Titanium White using the ¼-inch rake brush. Start on the bottom front of the left hand and follow the contour of the hand, making vertical and horizontal strokes. Do the same for the other hand. Brush a little Soft Black from the back of each hand toward the front. To finish the hands, add two or three lines, following the contour of the hand, to indicate finger separation.

Paint the Rabbit's Fur

Create the rabbit fur with short strokes. Paint the fur using a ¼-inch rake brush loaded consecutively with Soft Black, Raw Umber, Mink Tan, Toffee, Buttermilk and a little Titanium White. Clean your brush in between colors. Following the fur growth guide on page 49, paint the lighter colors on the back, the left side of the forehead, a little on the right forearm and more on the left forearm. Do not use much of the lighter colors as they will overpower the rabbit. Paint the darker fur on the right side, especially on the forelegs and on the right edge of the rabbit.

Keep the fur short and follow the growth guide; this will give the rabbit its roundness. If the rabbit is too light or too dark for your taste, increase the opposite colors. Finally, to indicate shadow, load your rake brush with a little French Grey Blue and add some fur to the right side of his forehead, on the right ear, on the back of his right arm and on the right side of his belly. This should be very subtle.

Highlight the rabbit's eyes with a liner brush tipped in Titanium White. The highlighting goes toward the back of the eye.

Basecoat the Roses and Leaves

Basecoat the roses with Titanium White. You'll need to apply two or three coats to get a nice even coverage. Basecoat the leaves and the rosebuds with Antique Green. Use Raw Umber to basecoat the main stems and Antique Green to basecoat the stems leading to the rosebuds. Reapply the pattern details with dark graphite.

❦ **HINT** ❧ *Don't press too hard when reapplying the pattern. The lines on the flowers should be barely visible.*

Shading and Highlighting Placement Guide

© DAKOTA '98

Highlight the Leaves and Stems

For the first highlight on the leaves, use a no. 6 filbert brush loaded with Dried Basil Green. Highlight the stems with the no. 0 liner brush sideloaded with Mink Tan. Make vertical strokes randomly on the stem. Keep in mind the position of your light source and where the shadows will fall on the opposite side.

For the second highlight on the leaves, use a no. 4 filbert brush (which is a size smaller than the first highlight brush) sideloaded with Cool Neutral. Go over the first highlights. Highlight the stems with a no. 0 liner brush loaded with Toffee using the same vertical strokes. Add a tiny bit of Titanium White to the liner brush for the final highlight on the rosebuds, the calyx and the curled leaves.

Shade the Leaves and Roses

Float the Antique Green and Raw Umber mix sideloaded on a no. 6 flat into all the shaded areas of the leaves, according to the placement guide (see page 52). For the second shading, use the Antique Green and Soft Black mixture. Sideload a no. 6 flat with this mixture, and go over the first shading in the deepest shadow areas—where leaves go under leaves, under one of the flowers or under a leaf curl.

> ❧ HINT ❧ *Add the second shading to only some of the leaves; this will create variety and interest.*

Using Cool Neutral sideloaded on the no. 6 flat, shade the roses where the petals curl back, usually on the outside edges. On the newly opened buds, shade the background petal and the bottom. Highlight with Titanium White if needed.

Finish the Rose

Paint the rose center with a no. 6 filbert brush sideloaded with Antique Gold. Use Cadmium Yellow loaded on a no. 4 filbert brush to paint the very center. With either your stylus or the liner brush, randomly place dots of Cadmium Yellow, Antique Gold and Raw Sienna in the Antique Gold area.

To make the rose a little more realistic, add a small float of Raw Sienna on a few edges using the no. 6 flat. Don't add too much or it will overpower the rose. Load a dirty liner brush with thinned Soft Black, and outline the leaves of the rose buds and parts of some of the rose petals.

Add the Final Touches

Add a few tufts of grass around the rabbit to anchor it into the scene. Using the rake or no. 6 flat brush, paint the blades of grass first with Antique Green, then Dried Basil Green and Cool Neutral, overlapping the strokes to create a full tuft of grass. Varnish the entire desk with J.W. etc. Right-Step Satin Varnish, as described on page 13.

Twins (Fawns)

While on a horseback ride in the mountains of northern New Mexico, I came across these two little deer. Little did I know at the time how foretelling this event would be. Before long I gave birth to my own twins. They are two beautiful individuals with just a hint of mischief about them. Because of my twins, I have a special affection for this project, and I tried my best to impart a little of each of my twins' personalities into these fawns.

Deer can be found almost anywhere there is a thicket and trees. You'll see them most often at twilight or in the early morning hours as the sun is coming up, feeding on grasses.

Materials List

SUPPLIES:
preparation supplies
  (see page 12)
general supplies
  (see page 13)
finishing supplies
  (see page 13)
DecoArt Faux Glazing medium
cheesecloth
Winsor & Newton Burnt
  Umber oil paint

BRUSHES:
no. 0 liner
no. 4, no. 6 rounds
no. 4, no. 8 filberts
¼-inch, ½-inch rakes
no. 4, no. 6, no.10 , ⅜-inch,
  ½-inch, 1-inch flats
1-inch sponge

SURFACE:
twig bench from
  Crews Country Pleasures

DecoArt Americana Acrylic Paints

| Hi-Lite Flesh | Base Flesh | French Mocha | Titanium White | Buttermilk |

| French Vanilla | True Ochre | Jade Green | Hauser Medium Green | Plantation Pine |

| Dove Grey | Graphite | Lamp Black | Raw Umber | Honey Brown |

| Light Cinnamon | Burnt Orange | Burnt Sienna | Russet | Burnt Umber | Plantation Pine + Raw Umber (1:1) |

Pattern

This pattern may be hand-traced or photo-copied for personal use only. Enlarge to 200 percent to bring to size for this project.

Shading and Highlighting Placement Guide

Prepare the Surface and Basecoat the Fawns

To keep this piece looking very natural, prepare and seal the surface as explained on page 11, but do not basecoat. Antique the edges with Burnt Umber acrylic paint plus Faux Glazing medium.

Apply the pattern with graphite paper and a stylus. Basecoat the fawns Honey Brown using a no. 10 flat brush, or any brush you feel comfortable using. Basecoat the trillium leaves with Hauser Medium Green and the flowers with Buttermilk. When dry, retrace the interior lines of the fawns, leaves and flowers. Basecoat the ears with a no. 6 round brush loaded with Base Flesh.

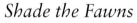

Shade the Fawns

Shade the fawns first with Light Cinnamon sideloaded on a ⅜-inch flat brush. Refer to the placement guide on page 58 for where to place the shading. Use Russet as the second shading color, sideloading it on a no. 6 flat. The smaller brush allows you to cover a slightly smaller area so you get a nice gradation of shades. Add the final shading at the very end of the project.

Painting the Eyes

STEP 1: You don't need to add a lot of detail to the eyes because these fawns are not very close to you. If something is close to the viewer, it needs more detail than if it is far away. Basecoat the eyes with Raw Umber.

STEP 2: Shade the top of the eye with a no. 4 flat brush sideloaded with Lamp Black. The shading should be about two-thirds of the way down the eye.

STEP 3: Load a no. 0 liner brush with Lamp Black to outline the eye. To complete the eye, use the liner to put a highlight dot of Buttermilk in the corner of the eye at about two o'clock for the right eye and ten o'clock for the left eye.

Painting the Ears

STEP 1: Basecoat the inside of the ears with Base Flesh.

STEP 2: Shade the ears with a no. 4 flat brush sideloaded with French Mocha. Brush the shading toward the outside edge of the ear without covering the base color. This begins to show the fur direction. Add a second shading with Russet sideloaded on the no. 4 flat brush.

Look at the placement guide on page for shading and highlighting positions. Highlight the inside of the ear using the no. 4 flat sideloaded with Hi-Lite Flesh. Brush the highlight toward the inside edge of the ear, indicating fur direction.

STEP 3: Young fawns do not have ear fur as long as the adult deer's. Using a ½-inch rake brush, indicate fur on the outside edges of the ear with Buttermilk, Raw Umber on the opposite edges and Russet to indicate the fur direction. Clean the brush after each color. Continue to alternate colors until you are satisfied with the fur.

 HINT *When using a rake brush, thin the paint to an inky consistency with water.*

Highlight the Fawns

Most of the highlights on the fawns are done when painting the fur. However, there are a few areas that have a slightly heavier highlight. With a ½-inch flat sideloaded with Buttermilk, highlight the left-hand fawn's chest, around its leg, the top of the head and the nose. On the fawn on the right, highlight slightly on the neck and nose.

❧ **HINT** ❧ *If the highlight is too bright, lower the intensity with a wash of Honey Brown.*

Painting the Muzzle

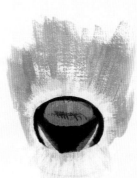

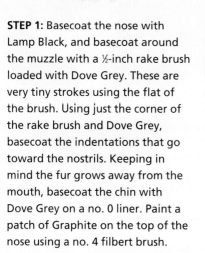

STEP 1: Basecoat the nose with Lamp Black, and basecoat around the muzzle with a ½-inch rake brush loaded with Dove Grey. These are very tiny strokes using the flat of the brush. Using just the corner of the rake brush and Dove Grey, basecoat the indentations that go toward the nostrils. Keeping in mind the fur grows away from the mouth, basecoat the chin with Dove Grey on a no. 0 liner. Paint a patch of Graphite on the top of the nose using a no. 4 filbert brush.

STEP 2: Next, using the rake brush loaded with Buttermilk, rake small wisps of fur away from the nose. Do not cover all of the basecoat color. Shade the chin with the same color using longer strokes. Highlight along the top of the nose using a no. 6 round loaded with Graphite.

STEP 3: Using the rake brush loaded with Titanium White, put the final highlight in the fur over the nose and on the chin. Create a wash of Lamp Black, and wash it over the Graphite on the nose. Place the final highlight of Titanium White on the nose. After both have dried, create a wash of Dove Grey and wash the lower part of the Graphite section.

Load the rake with Graphite, and shade the fur above the nose, to the right of the nose and on the right side of the chin.

Sideload a no. 4 flat brush with Raw Umber. Float a shadow around the nose, especially on the dark side. If you get too much shadow on the light side of the nose, go back over the fur with the rake brush loaded with Buttermilk or Titanium White.

Paint the Fur

Using a ¼-inch rake brush, paint the fur with French Vanilla, Titanium White, Burnt Sienna and Burnt Orange, all thinned with water. Rinse the brush after each color. Refer to the picture above for placement. Brush French Vanilla on the forehead; notice in the picture above that the hair grows in almost a *V* formation. Highlight under the chin with French Vanilla, making a tuft of white fur. Go over this same area with a little Titanium White. Add a little brush of French Vanilla around the black part of the nose. Adjust the face as you see fit until you get a nice transition of colors.

Add a little Graphite in small dashes across the cheeks.

With a ¼-inch rake, brush a few small fur marks on the fawns' backs, first with Burnt Sienna and next with Burnt Orange as a highlight. Both fawns are primarily done the same way and with the same colors. Refer to the picture above for the fur placement. If you paint the fur too thick or you don't like the color, you can always lower the intensity with a little Raw Umber or add more of one of the other colors. Make sure you blend the color smoothly with the rake.

Paint the Spots

Use either a no. 4 filbert or a liner brush to dab or stroke on the spots. Make sure each color dries before you add more color. Start painting the spots with French Vanilla, then add Buttermilk to most of the spots. Highlight a few spots with Titanium White. The spots are put on in a slightly random pattern. If you don't like the way the spots look, you can tone them down with a bit of Burnt Sienna or brighten them with a little more Titanium White.

Paint the Leaves and Flowers

Basecoat the leaves with Hauser Medium Green and the flowers with Buttermilk.

Shade the leaves with a no. 8 filbert sideloaded with Plantation Pine. Clean the filbert and sideload it with Jade Green. Place an oval highlight down the middle and on the opposite edge of the full leaves. Refer to the final picture on page 67 for the shading and highlighting areas of the different leaves. With a no. 4 round loaded with True Ochre, dab in the center of the flowers. Shade around the center and edges of the flower petals with a brush mix of Jade Green and Buttermilk loaded on a 1-inch flat. Use this same mixture to shade where petals overlap each other or where they overlap leaves.

Shade the flower centers with dabs of Burnt Sienna loaded on a no. 4 round. Shade the leaves with a no. 6 flat brush sideloaded with the Plantation Pine and Raw Umber mix, shading over the same areas shaded with Plantation Pine. Add vein lines to the leaves with Jade Green loaded on a no. 0 liner brush.

Paint the Grapevines

Paint the grapevines with a long bristle liner brush loaded with thinned Raw Umber. In this demonstration, I used a no. 4 round brush, but you should use the brush that is most appropriate for the size surface you've decided to use. Paint the vines all around the surface about 1 inch in from the edge.

After the basecoat, use a little Lamp Black to shade the vines and Buttermilk to highlight the vines. Do this in a random pattern to give it a more realistic appearance.

Paint the Large Border Leaves

STEP 1: Doubleload a 1-inch flat brush with Plantation Pine and Jade Green. Starting on the chisel edge of the brush, press down on the bristles and begin to wiggle the brush back and forth as you turn and come back to the chisel edge. The Jade Green side of the brush can face the inside or the outside of the leaf.

STEP 2: Repeat the previous stroke for the opposite side of the leaf. Place either the Plantation Pine, for shading, or Jade Green, for highlighting, on the outside of the leaf. Add vein lines using a no. 0 liner brush loaded with Plantation Pine.

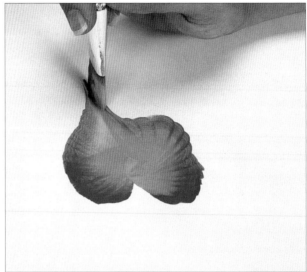

Paint the Small Border Leaves

To create smaller, one-stroke leaves, doubleload the 1-inch flat with Plantation Pine and Jade Green. Starting on the chisel edge, press down on the bristles, turn and lift back to the chisel. Place these randomly around the border.

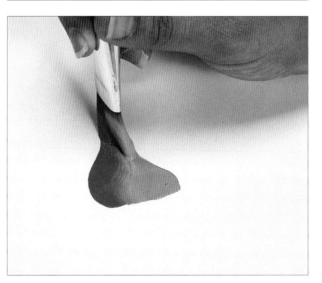

Add the Final Touches

Shade around the inside of the vine with Burnt Umber sideloaded on a 1-inch flat brush. With Burnt Umber on a no. 10 flat, shade the fawns where the leaves overlap them.

Seal the painting with two coats of J.W. etc. Right-Step Satin Varnish. Then, add antiquing with Burnt Umber oil paint on a cheesecloth. If you'd like to add coats of varnish over the antiquing, wait about three weeks to ensure the oil paint has dried.

Free (Wild Horses)

Horses have always been an important part of my life—from riding horses at my grandfather's farm as a little girl to riding in the mountains of northern New Mexico as an adult. I once witnessed a group of eight domestic horses running across a two-hundred-acre pasture right toward me. Mother Nature was very alive to me at that moment. I can still hear the thunder of their hoof beats and hear their whinnying sounds of delight. It brings me chills thinking about the sight of their manes and tails billowing in the wind. At that moment those eight horses were as free as any wild horse.

This incredible scene has stuck in my mind for years—I had never been so aware of nature's power. I have finally painted that moment and included my favorite horse, the Painted Pony. I hope you can feel the awesome power I felt that day when you paint this scene for yourself.

Materials List

SUPPLIES:
preparation supplies
  (see page 12)
general supplies
  (see page 13)
finishing supplies
  (see page 13)
graining tool
DecoArt Faux Glazing medium
sea sponge
no. 2 pencil

BRUSHES:
no. 0 liner
no. 4, no. 6 rounds
no. 6, no. 8, no. 10 filberts
¼-inch rake
no. 4, no. 8, no. 10, 1-inch flats
scruffy
1-inch or 2-inch sponge

SURFACE:
high-backed bench was a
  flea market find

DecoArt Americana Acrylic Paints

Slate Grey	Soft Black	Buttermilk	True Ochre	Titanium White

Mississippi Mud	Milk Chocolate	Burnt Umber	Antique White	Russet

Burnt Sienna	Napa Red	Camel	White Wash

Mississippi Mud + Burnt Umber (1:1)	Mississippi Mud + Soft Black (1:1)	Milk Chocolate + Antique White (1:1)	Milk Chocolate + Burnt Umber (1:1)	Milk Chocolate + Soft Black (1:1)

Patterns

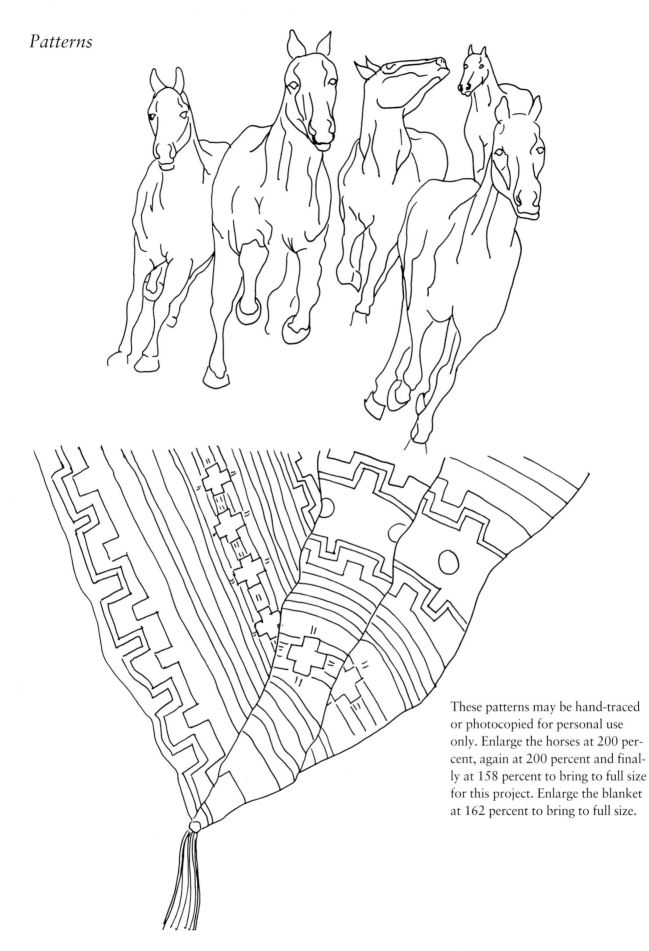

These patterns may be hand-traced or photocopied for personal use only. Enlarge the horses at 200 percent, again at 200 percent and finally at 158 percent to bring to full size for this project. Enlarge the blanket at 162 percent to bring to full size.

These patterns may be hand-traced or photocopied for personal use only. To bring the images to full size for this project, enlarge the horseshoe and nail at 120 percent, the feather at 133 percent and the rope at 200 percent.

Paint the Wood Grain

Paint the bench sides and seat with Slate Grey. Let dry thoroughly, about twenty-four hours. Prepare approximately one-half cup of Soft Black and Faux Glazing medium mix (2:1). With a sponge brush, apply the glaze mixture thinly over the Slate Grey.

Using the graining tool, pull down the length of the surface, rocking the tool forward and backward as you slide it toward you. Do not pull straight down without rocking the tool as this won't make the desired wood grain effect. The graining tool may be purchased at home centers and craft stores.

Create the Torn Parchment

Basecoat the seat back and front panel with Buttermilk. Dampen a sea sponge, load with True Ochre and tap it out on a paper towel. Working in a small area, start tapping True Ochre in the corners of the surface and work toward the center. Before it dries, use a paper towel or soft cloth to rub the True Ochre toward the center so the color is darker around the edges and lighter in the center. Let dry.

Using a no. 2 pencil, lightly sketch a ragged oval around the area in which you will paint the horses. Lightly sketch the torn and curled edges, referring to the image above for placement.

To create the turned-over corners, sideload a no. 10 flat brush with True Ochre, floating the color on what would be the back of the curled parchment. Shade the darkest areas with Milk Chocolate sideloaded on a no. 10 flat. Now, load a no. 0 liner brush with thinned Milk Chocolate, and add a thin line on the edge of the curled and torn parchment. Highlight the centers of the tears and a few edges with thinned Buttermilk and then thinned Titanium White loaded on a no. 4 flat. Remember the light is coming from the front and left side.

Now apply the horse pattern in the open center of the torn parchment.

Basecoat the Horses

The Two-Horse Grouping

With a no. 10 flat brush, basecoat the horse on the left with Mississippi Mud thinned with a little bit of water. Basecoat the horse on the right with thinned Milk Chocolate.

The Three-Horse Grouping

Use thinned Buttermilk loaded on the no. 10 flat to basecoat the foreground horse. Basecoat the horse on the left and background horse with thinned Milk Chocolate. After basecoating all the horses, reapply the details, if necessary, using white graphite paper and a stylus.

Milk Chocolate +
Burnt Umber

Mississippi Mud +
Burnt Umber

Mississippi Mud +
Soft Black

Milk Chocolate +
Soft Black

Antique White +
Mississippi Mud

Soft Black

Mississippi Mud

Shade the Horses

The Two-Horse Grouping

Referring to the image at left, shade the left-hand horse using a no. 8 filbert brush fully loaded first with a mixture of Mississippi Mud and Burnt Umber, thinned with a little bit of water. Then, shade the horse with a mixture of Mississippi Mud and Soft Black. Use pure Soft Black to deepen the darkest shadows.

Shade the horse on the right, first with a mixture of Milk Chocolate and Burnt Umber, thinned with a little bit of water. Next, shade using a mixture of Milk Chocolate and Soft Black. Deepen the shadows with pure Soft Black.

Paint the horses' eyes with Soft Black. Using a flattened no. 4 round brush sideloaded with Soft Black, make a small upside-down comma stroke toward the outside edge of the nostril.

Shade the hooves with Burnt Umber on a ¼-inch rake. Keep in mind, however, that the hooves will be mostly covered by dust clouds painted around the legs later.

The Three-Horse Grouping

Shade the two background horses exactly like the right-hand horse in the two-horse grouping; refer to the image at left for placement.

Shade the dun-colored horse in the foreground with a no. 8 flat loaded with a brush mix of Antique White and Mississippi Mud thinned with a little bit of water. Next, shade using straight Mississippi Mud, then with Soft Black.

❧ **HINT** ❧ *Use Soft Black sparingly on this horse or it will be very overpowering.*

Paint the eyes, nostrils and hooves as described for the two-horse grouping.

Highlight the Horses

The Two-Horse Grouping

Referring to the image at right, highlight the left-hand horse with Antique White, then with Buttermilk. Finally, with Titanium White, highlight randomly on the left side of the left-hand horse. The spot on his forehead is a mixture of Buttermilk and Mississippi Mud. For the mane, load a liner brush with Soft Black, and, starting at the horse's neck, make wavy strokes as if the mane is blowing in the wind. Add individual hairs with the liner brush loaded with Antique White.

Highlight the horse on the right first with a mixture of Milk Chocolate and Antique White on a no. 8 filbert. Next, reinforce the highlight with Buttermilk. On the left side of the horse, highlight sparingly with Titanium White so as not to overpower the other colors. Paint the mane as described above.

The Three-Horse Grouping

Highlight the background horse only slightly, first with Buttermilk and then with Titanium White. Highlight the horse on the left with Buttermilk as shown at right.

Highlight the foreground horse with the Antique White and Buttermilk mix. Thin the mixture with a little bit of water. Reinforce the highlight with pure Buttermilk. The final highlight is Titanium White.

Paint all the horses' manes with Soft Black and Antique White as described in the two-horse grouping.

Adjust the colors as you see fit, adding lighter colors if the horses are too dark and darker colors if they're too light.

Antique White

Buttermilk

Milk Chocolate + Antique White

Buttermilk

Buttermilk

Buttermilk

Titanium White

Antique White + Buttermilk

76

Finish the Horses

The Two-Horse Grouping

To make the Milk Chocolate horse of the two-horse grouping a pinto, add splotches of thinned White Wash with a no.6 round. Don't add too much of the White.

To finish this scene, add the dust from the running horses with White Wash and Burnt Umber sideloaded on a scruffy brush. Scumble and pounce in a random pattern starting at the horses' hind legs. See page 83 for a picture of the complete dust cloud.

The Three-Horse Grouping

Paint dust around the horses, as described above.

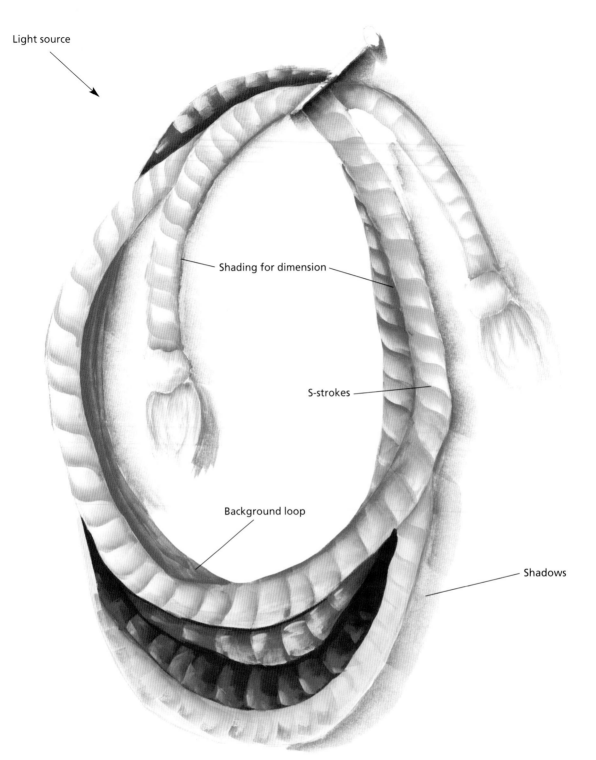

Light source

Shading for dimension

S-strokes

Background loop

Shadows

Paint the Rope

To create the texture of the rope, paint S-stroke after S-stroke on the outside rope loop using a no. 10 flat brush loaded with Antique White. Paint the S-strokes on the background loops with progressively darker colors, including Mississippi Mud and Soft Black, for a three-dimensional look. With a no. 8 flat brush highlight the rope with Buttermilk and then with Titanium White on the side where the light is coming from—in this case from the left. Paint the shadow with Soft Black thinned with water on the no. 10 flat, following the illustration above for placement.

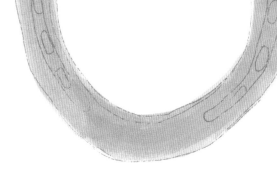

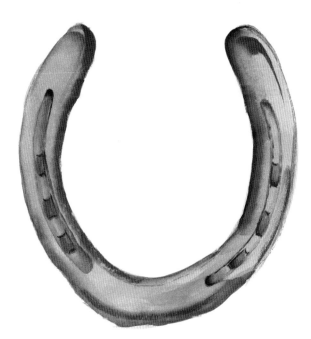

Paint the Horseshoe and Rusty Nail

Undercoat the horseshoe with Titanium White. Then basecoat it with thinned Milk Chocolate and let dry.

Shade the horseshoe with a no. 10 filbert brush sideloaded with Russet and Burnt Umber consecutively.

To create the rusty look, add a little thinned Burnt Sienna and Soft Black randomly to the horseshoe with a no. 8 filbert brush. Then, highlight the horseshoe with Buttermilk, Titanium White and True Ochre using a no. 6 dry round brush; do not load too much color on the brush. Create the shadow with a no. 10 filbert brush loaded with Soft Black thinned a lot with water. Follow these same procedures for painting the nail.

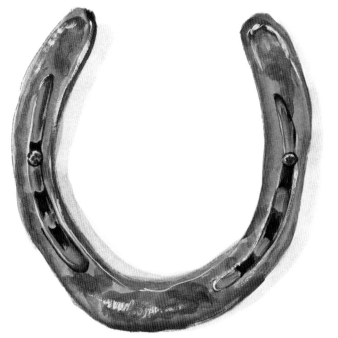

Paint the Navajo Saddle Blanket

STEP 1: Basecoat the blanket with a 1-inch flat brush loaded with Napa Red. Apply the paint in a diagonal direction. In this case, it's OK to have the brush marks show. Don't make a solid basecoat.

STEP 2: Reapply the details of the blanket pattern. You may want to use white transfer paper so you can see the lines more clearly. Use True Ochre, Buttermilk and Soft Black to solidly paint the patterns, loading each on a no. 6 round brush. Make sure you clean the brush between colors. Refer to the images at right for color placement.

STEP 3: To finish the blanket, add shadows using a large flat brush sideloaded with Soft Black. Follow each outside edge where the blanket rolls. Also, shade on the left side of the blanket for a cast shadow with thinned Soft Black sideloaded on a large flat brush. Highlight the center section of the blanket with a very thin wash of Buttermilk, and blot with a paper towel or cheesecloth.

Paint the Feather

STEP 1: First, undercoat the feather with two coats of Titanium White. Basecoat the feather with Antique White and the feather shaft with Buttermilk. Basecoat the leather braid with Camel. After the basecoat has dried, reapply the pattern details.

STEP 2: Shade the feather with Mississippi Mud using a no. 8 flat brush. Place the shading on the outside and inside edges of the large side. When this has dried, use a ¼-inch rake loaded with thinned Mississippi Mud and stroke in toward the shaft from the outside edge of the short side. Brush from the shaft toward the outside edge of the larger side. To create the individual feathers, use a no. 0 liner brush loaded with thinned Milk Chocolate.

STEP 3: To highlight, use the ¼-inch rake brush loaded with a little thinned Buttermilk and brush from the outside toward the shaft. Highlight the shaft with Titanium White using a no. 0 liner brush. Add the feather stripes using a no. 6 filbert brush loaded with Milk Chocolate, stroking back and forth in the pattern area. Shade the leather braid with True Ochre and Milk Chocolate. Paint the feather's shadow with a 1-inch flat sideloaded with thinned Soft Black.

Paint the Stylized Horses
There are three stylized horses on
the front panel of the bench's seat.
Paint them solidly with Soft Black,
True Ochre and Titanium White.

Finish the Project
Varnish the bench as directed on
page 13 using matte or satin
varnish.

The completed bench.

Lazy Summer Days (Grizzly Bear)

While living in a tipi, I once had a misadventure with a brown bear. I think he was more afraid of me than I was of him—or maybe I didn't have time to think about it. I've always been fascinated with bears; they seem so carefree and happy. They have such raw power and yet have a certain wisdom and gentleness about them.

Brown bears are my favorite type of bear, including the great grizzly, which got its name because of its grizzly fur. My next adventure will surely take me to visit the grizzlies of the Northwest.

Materials List

SUPPLIES:
preparation supplies
  (see page 12)
general supplies
  (see page 13)
finishing supplies
  (see page 13)
DecoArt Brush 'n Blend
  Extender
brown paper bag, crumpled

BRUSHES:
no. 0 liner
no. 6 round
no. 6 filbert
¼-inch rake
no. 8, 1-inch flats
large, stiff scruffy

SURFACE:
place mat box from
  Woodcrafts

DecoArt Americana Acrylic Paints

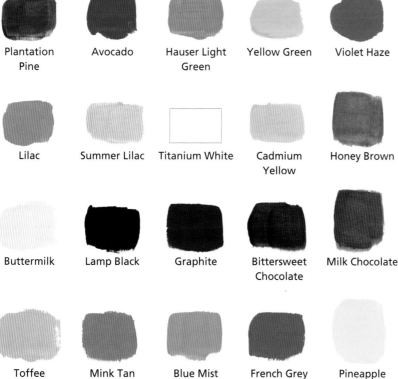

Plantation Pine · Avocado · Hauser Light Green · Yellow Green · Violet Haze

Lilac · Summer Lilac · Titanium White · Cadmium Yellow · Honey Brown

Buttermilk · Lamp Black · Graphite · Bittersweet Chocolate · Milk Chocolate

Toffee · Mink Tan · Blue Mist · French Grey Blue · Pineapple

Pattern

This pattern may be hand-traced or
photocopied for personal use only.
Enlarge to 200 percent to bring to
size for this project.

Paint the Background

Coat your unsealed surface with Brush 'n Blend Extender medium so it has a nice shine. Load a 1-inch flat brush with Blue Mist. Starting at the top of your surface, paint long strokes across and one-third of the way down your surface. Add some Buttermilk to your dirty brush, and continue down your surface with the same long horizontal strokes, picking up more Buttermilk as you go.

If your brush dries out or the paint becomes sticky, pick up more blending medium. Let the basecoat dry for at least one hour. Then sand lightly with a crumpled brown paper bag.

Load a large, stiff scruffy brush with Plantation Pine. Pounce the brush on your palette to remove excess paint, then pounce up and down on the Buttermilk side of the surface, following the contours of the box. Leave about 1-inch at the edge. Add more paint as you feel necessary.

Paint the background grass with a no. 8 flat brush loaded with Plantation Pine, using the chisel edge to make choppy strokes. Let dry, then apply the pattern with graphite paper and a stylus.

Basecoat the Bear

Basecoat the bear with Mink Tan using your favorite basecoating brush. Basecoat the bear's muzzle with Toffee and his nose and irises with Graphite.

Shading and Highlighting Placement Guide

Fur Growth Guide

Painting the Muzzle

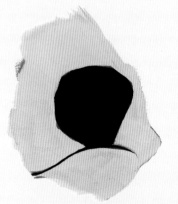

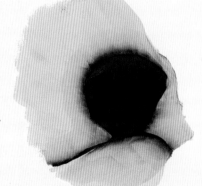

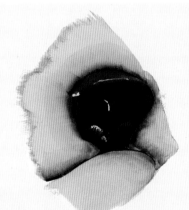

STEP 1: Basecoat the muzzle with Toffee and the nose with Graphite.

STEP 2: With a no. 6 filbert brush, create highlights on the nose, as indicated in the image above, with a sideload of French Grey Blue. Shade around the nose and under the mouth with Graphite on the no. 6 filbert.

STEP 3: With Buttermilk loaded on a no. 0 liner, highlight the muzzle and top of the nose. Highlight lightly with Titanium White.

Shade the Bear

Reapply the details of the bear. Shade the bear with Graphite around the nose and mouth using a no. 8 flat. Shade the cheeks and forehead using a no. 6 filbert side-loaded with Bittersweet Chocolate, creating back-to-back floats. Shade the ears first with Bittersweet Chocolate and then with Graphite using the no. 8 flat.

❧ HINT ❧ The darkest shade in the ears should be closest to the head.

Shade the body with floats of Bittersweet Chocolate. With the no. 8 flat brush, add a little Milk Chocolate in an inky consistency around the left eye, down the left cheek and on the bear's back. Using only the chisel end of the brush, make choppy marks to indicate fur direction (see guide at left). This will create the general dark fur.

Painting the Eyes

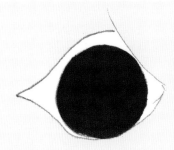

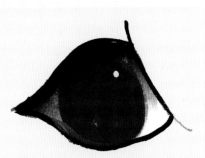

STEP 1: Basecoat the iris with Graphite.

STEP 2: Shade the eye with a no. 6 filbert sideloaded with Lamp Black. Outline the entire eye using a no. 0 liner brush loaded with Lamp Black.

STEP 3: Using the no. 0 liner loaded with Honey Brown, add a small comma stroke on the bottom of the iris. Load the liner brush with Buttermilk, and make a dot for the eye highlight. Because the light source is from the left, make the highlight in the left eye heavier than the highlight in the right eye.

Highlight the Bear

The highlights on the bear are created as you apply the fur. Use either a ¼-inch rake brush or, for the final details, a no. 0 liner brush to paint all the highlights. With your brush loaded with Toffee and later Buttermilk, place the highlights according to the placement guide on page 88.

❧ HINT ❧ *The fur direction will make all the difference as to whether your bear looks real, so refer to the growth direction drawing on page 88 often.*

Finish the Bear

When you've completed the highlights, add more individual hairs using all the colors of the bear. In some of the highlight areas, place some darker hairs. In the darker areas, place some highlight hairs. However, don't make them stand out too much; use the next darker or lighter shade as the case may be.

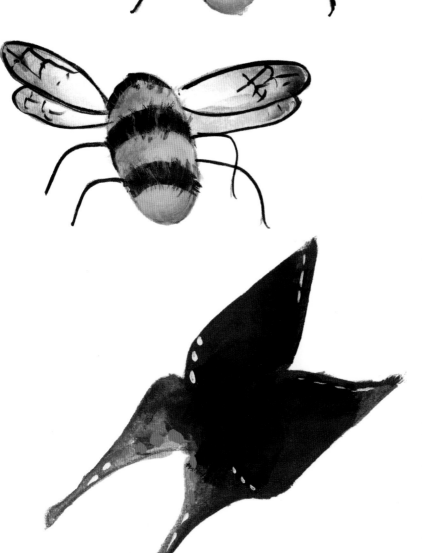

Paint the Bees and Butterfly

Bees

Base the rings of the bees alternating Cadmium Yellow and Lamp Black.

Next, shade the wings with a no. 6 filbert sideloaded with Graphite. Load Honey Brown on a no. 0 liner to shade the yellow part of the body. With a no. 0 liner brush and Lamp Black, create the legs and outline the wings. You can use a permanent marker for this if it feels more comfortable.

With the liner, add a few small crosshatches to give the wings texture. Using the rake brush, create bee fur using Cadmium Yellow and Lamp Black. The bees are far away from the viewer, so don't feel you have to spend a lot of time adding details.

Butterfly

You can use a variety of colors to paint the butterfly. I decided to make a swallowtail using a no. 6 filbert loaded with Lamp Black. Paint the details with Blue Mist loaded on a no. 0 liner. The butterfly is far away so there is not much detail. Follow the close-up view at left for color placement.

Paint Blades of Grass and the Stump

Blades of Grass

Paint the grass using a no. 8 flat brush loaded with Avocado. When your basecoat has dried, load the same clean brush with Plantation Pine. Using the chisel edge of the brush, chop in the shadows on the underside of the grass blade. Use the same method to apply the highlights, first using Hauser Light Green and then Yellow Green. Do not use too much Yellow Green or it will overwhelm the grass blade.

Tree Stump

Basecoat the tree with Mink Tan; you can do this when you basecoa the bear. Basecoat the hole in the tree with Bittersweet Chocolate. Shade the bottom of the trunk wit Bittersweet Chocolate using a 1-inch flat brush. Shade the triangle where the trunk bends with Bittersweet Chocolate on the 1-inch flat Shade the hole using the flat brush sideloaded with Lamp Black. High light the top of the trunk using the same flat brush sideloaded with Buttermilk. To make the bark, make random vertical choppy marks on the trunk with Buttermilk, Toffee and Bittersweet Chocolate using the 1-inch flat brush. Clean the brush in between colors.

Paint the Leaves

Paint the leaves using a no. 8 flat brush loaded with Avocado. Starting on the outside edge, make an S-stroke toward the center. Make as many S-strokes as will fill that side of the leaf. Repeat to create the other side of the leaf.

Now, sideload a no. 8 flat with Plantation Pine, and shade one-half of the leaf in the center. Which half you shade depends on where your light source is coming from; in this project, I've shaded the right side of the leaves.

Using the same, cleaned brush sideloaded with Hauser Light Green, highlight the leaf on its edges. Add the veins with a no. 0 liner brush loaded with Hauser Light Green.

For the small leaves, load a no. 6 round brush with Avocado. Starting on the outside edge, press down and pull toward the stem as you slowly lift the brush back to a point. With a no. 0 liner brush loaded with Avocado, paint the stem.

Add character to the closer leaves by adding Evergreen and Hauser Light Green randomly to each leaf. For the leaves in the background, randomly basecoat with Evergreen and Avocado.

Paint the Flowers

Daisies

With a no. 8 flat brush sideloaded with Blue Mist, shade around the center of each daisy. Let this dry.

Basecoat the centers with Cadmium Yellow. Use a no. 6 round brush loaded with Titanium White to make the petals. Holding the brush straight up and down, start on the tip, push down to spread the bristles, then slide the brush toward the center, lifting as you go. End on the tip.

Shade the centers using a no. 6 filbert sideloaded with Honey Brown, then add a little more Honey Brown to the centers by pouncing in with a scruffy brush. Using a no. 0 liner brush or stylus loaded with Lamp Black, add some dots to the centers. Do not make all the daisies the same shape. Vary the sizes and shapes of your daisies, using smaller brushes for the background flowers.

Chicory

Load a no. 6 round with Violet Haze, and, beginning at the outside, paint the chicory petals, gradually lifting the brush as you approach the blooms' centers. A no. 0 liner brush will work well for the chicory in the background.

Following the same method as described above, paint the top layers of petals with Summer Lilac. Place these petals so that some of the bottom petals show through.

Highlight the petals by brushing lightly with a ¼-inch rake brush loaded with Lilac. Load a liner brush with Cadmium Yellow, and paint a few short, choppy lines in each center. Finally, with the liner brush and Violet Haze, paint wavy lines for the stamens.

94

Sundrops

Basecoat the sundrops with Cadmium Yellow.

Highlight the petals using a no. 6 filbert sideloaded with Pineapple. Add a few lines with a no. 0 liner brush loaded with thinned Honey Brown, then for the center, add a dot of Avocado with the liner brush. Again, don't make the flowers all the same. Add some variety by using different shades of yellow or by presenting flowers at different angles.

Finish the Project

Apply two coats of J.W. etc. Right-Step Satin Varnish. Sand lightly with a very fine sanding pad dipped in soapy water. Apply several more coats of varnish, sanding lightly after each.

New Life (Wolf Pup)

Some friends of mine in New Mexico raise wolves. It was always exciting to wake up to the sound of the wolves howling or to listen to them at dusk. The sound always started out very soft and muted with just one wolf, and then gradually the entire pack would join in. It was so exhilarating, you almost wanted to join in yourself.

One spring the alpha female gave birth to pups. They were very cute (and destructive), but most of all, they were very curious about the world. Here's one little guy who doesn't quite want to leave the safety of the den.

Materials List

SUPPLIES:
preparation supplies
 (see page 12)
general supplies
 (see page 13)
finishing supplies
 (see page 13)

BRUSHES:
no. 0 liner
no. 6 round
½-inch stiff-bristle filbert
 (I used a brush for oils)
¼-inch rake
no. 8, 1-inch flats
small scruffy

SURFACE:
oval, slim bentwood box
 from Cabin Crafters

DecoArt Americana Acrylic Paints

Buttermilk Titanium White Pineapple Yellow Light Cadmium Yellow

Tangerine Green Mist Mint Julep Green Lamp Black Reindeer Moss Green

Light Avocado Avocado Black Green Payne's Grey Cashmere Beige

Mississippi Mud Raw Umber Soft Black Raw Sienna French Mocha

Patterns

These patterns may be hand-traced or photocopied for personal use only. Enlarge the wolf at 115 percent and the flowers and nest at 172 percent to bring to size for this project.

Basecoat Your Surface and Paint the Background

Basecoat the box and lid with Buttermilk. When this is completely dry (wait at least twenty-four hours), sand lightly. To paint the background mountains, load a large, stiff-bristle filbert brush with Payne's Grey thinned to an inky consistency. At about one-third of the way down the box, tap the brush at a 45° angle to the surface, a little here and there, to suggest distant mountains in the fog.

For the evergreen trees, add a touch of Black Green to the inky Payne's Grey. With the stiff-bristle brush, make a straight line down with the side of the brush, starting at the top of the tree. Then, tap in the branches, going from side to side on the tree with the flat of the brush at a 45° angle. As you move forward, painting trees that are closer to the viewer, paint the trees darker. If the trees are too dark, add a little more water to your mix. To add variety, make the evergreens different sizes.

Paint the Middle Ground

Beginning with Green Mist, paint the background bushes using the stiff-bristle brush, tapping and pushing the bristles away from you with the brush at a 45° angle. Below the Green Mist, add a layer of Mint Julep Green, then a layer of Reindeer Moss Green. These layers should reach about two-thirds of the way down the box. Below the Reindeer Moss Green, paint the underlayer of grass with Black Green, extending to the bottom of the side of the box.

Paint the Middle-Ground Bushes and Grass

Add slightly more detailed grass with Avocado, Light Avocado and Reindeer Moss Green by pushing upward on the stiff-bristle brush or a ¼-inch rake brush. Place the lighter colors toward the top. As you work downward, pick up the next color without cleaning your brush; this will help to blend the colors of the grass. You can also add lighter layers of color anywhere in the area to show patches of sunlight.

When all of this is dry and you're satisfied with the grass, bushes and background trees and mountains, clean your brush and load with a touch of thinned Buttermilk. With a a scrubbing, circular motion, make the fog more prominent in the mountains, between the trees and a little in the bushes.

Allow this to thoroughly dry, then apply the den pattern and black-eyed Susan pattern to the side of the box, making sure you apply the den pattern to the side without the seam. Repeat the black-eyed Susan pattern sparsely all around the sides of the box.

Paint the Trees

STEP 1: With a ½-inch filbert oil painting brush loaded with Black Green, make vertical lines of varying lengths for the trunks of the trees. Holding the same brush at a 45° angle to the surface, tap in the branches, moving back and forth across the bottom of the tree, moving slowly up trunk, tapering to a point at the top.

STEP 2: Wipe the brush with a damp paper towel and reload it with Avocado. Again, tap back and forth up the tree, taking care not to cover up the first color. This will complete the background trees.

STEP 3: Wipe the brush again with a damp paper towel, and load it with Jade Green. Tap back and forth on the trees that are to be in the foreground. On trees that overlap, tap Jade Green on the side that is in the foreground, leaving the receding side dark.

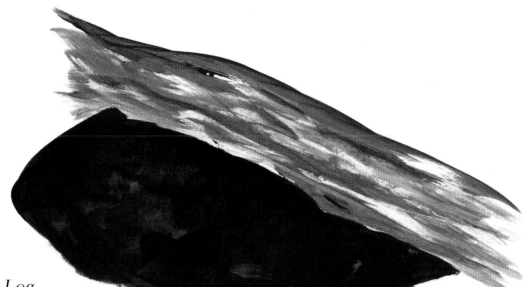

Basecoat the Log and Den

In this design, I've placed the den under a dead log and laid the wolf pup at the mouth of the den. Basecoat the mouth of the den with Soft Black, and basecoat the dead log with Raw Umber using a 1-inch flat brush.

Shade the Log and Den

Shade the log on the underside with Soft Black on the 1-inch flat. Using the chisel edge of your 1-inch flat, loaded with Raw Sienna, paint lines the length of the log. Add Mississippi Mud in choppy strokes along the log.

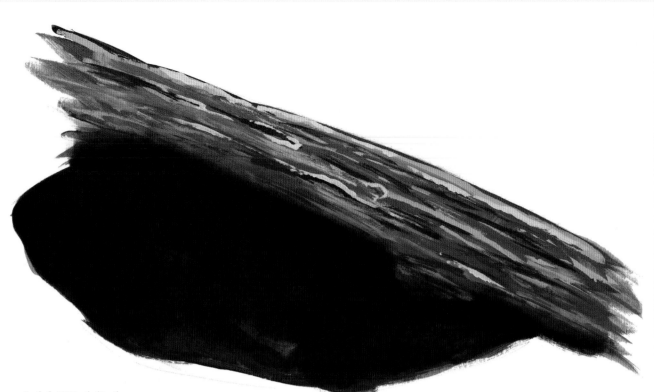

Add Highlights

Add touches of the Buttermilk over the Mississippi Mud with a 1-inch flat. The living tree trunks are painted the same way, but upright.

Darken the den hole under the log with a little Lamp Black using your 1-inch flat brush.

Paint the Moss

Tap in the moss using the no. 6 round brush loaded with Black Green. Let the moss cover some areas of the log, but leave others bare. Drape the moss down the sides of the log, too, keeping the placement natural and not symmetrical. Highlight the moss with Avocado and Reindeer Moss Green using the no. 6 round brush.

◆ HINT ◆ *Remember, the light is coming from the left side but is diffused by the fog. This means there won't be any heavy shadows. You can add a little fog in the foreground by applying a thin wash of Buttermilk over the tree trunks.*

Paint the Pine Branches

STEP 1: See page 115 for placement of the pine branches on lid and side of box. With a no. 0 liner brush loaded with Raw Umber, create the branches by making a straight line with some wiggles in it. The branch shouldn't be as squiggly as a vine. Split two branches off the tip of the main branch, and split several other branches off the sides of the main branch. Even the side branches should split into smaller branches.

With a ¼-inch rake brush loaded with Black Green, add needles, holding the brush at a 45° angle and pulling from the branch outward. Make the needles about ¼-inch long, but for variety some may be slightly longer and some shorter. This is a time-consuming process, so be patient.

STEP 2: Add more needles with the rake loaded with Avocado.

STEP 3: Highlight a few needles using a no. 0 liner brush loaded with Reindeer Moss Green and Mint Julep Green consecutively. The light source is coming from the left, so highlight the needles on the left side and a few on the right side that might catch some light.

Paint the Nest

STEP 1: With a 1-inch flat brush, basecoat the nest with Soft Black and the eggs with Buttermilk.

STEP 2: Shade the eggs with a sideload float of Raw Umber on the 1-inch flat. Clean the brush, then begin highlighting along the outside of the nest with Raw Umber.

STEP 3: Using a no. 0 liner brush, make crisscrosses of Mississippi Mud, Cashmere Beige and a little Buttermilk consecutively, to give the appearance of grass. Clean your brush after each color. Highlight the eggs with a back-to-back float of Titanium White on a no. 8 flat brush. Add speckles with thinned Soft Black spattered onto the eggs. With the liner brush loaded with thinned Mississippi Mud, paint the fine cracks on one of the eggs.

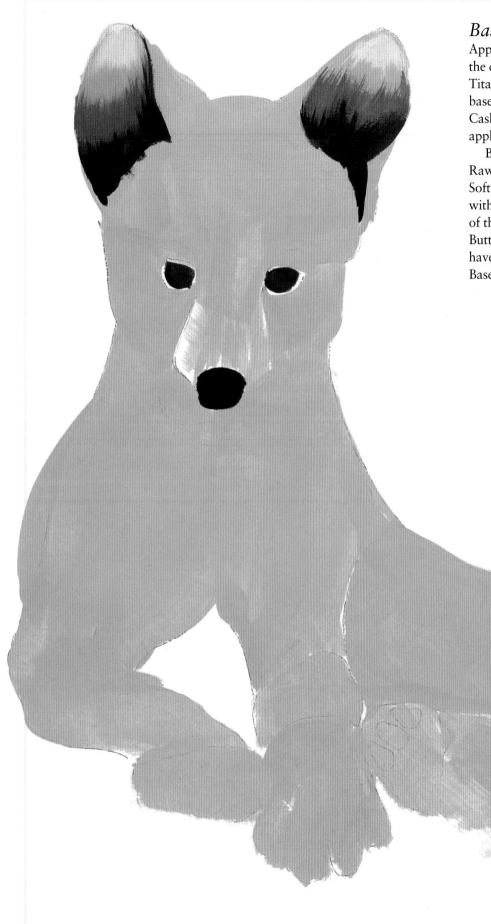

Basecoat the Wolf

Apply the basic wolf pup pattern by the den. Undercoat the wolf with Titanium White. Allow to dry, then basecoat the wolf's body with Cashmere Beige. Let dry, then re-apply the details of the pattern.

Basecoat the eyes with thinned Raw Umber. Basecoat the ears with Soft Black close to the head and with French Mocha toward the top of the ears. If you wish, add a little Buttermilk to the French Mocha to have the ear fade to a lighter color. Basecoat the nose with Soft Black.

Shade the Wolf

With Mississippi Mud sideloaded on a 1-inch flat brush, shade under the wolf's chin, on the right side of the nose, on the top of the head, around the chest area and down the back. If in doubt where to shade, refer to the picture at left.

Basecoat the foot pads with Soft Black loaded on a no. 6 round. (If you plan on adding a lot of grass around the wolf, painting the pads isn't necessary.)

While the ears are still wet from the basecoat, stroke Soft Black up toward the ear tip with the ¼-inch rake brush. Do not wash the brush.

Fur Growth Guide

Shading and Highlighting Placement Guide

Paint the Dark Fur

With your ¼-inch rake brush loaded with Raw Umber and Soft Black consecutively, paint the fur down the center of the muzzle, at the temples, on the top edge of the head, on the forehead (in a diamond shape), above the eyes, on the neck, down the forelegs and on the belly. Refer to the fur guide on page 110 for fur direction. Using a no. 8 flat, shade below the chin and around the haunches with Soft Black.

While the ears are still wet from the previous step, go back over the Soft Black with French Mocha and blend the colors with the rake brush, creating a gradation of color. The deepest shading should be near the head and along the right side of the right ear and along the left side of the left ear. If you need to re-apply the highlights, brush mix a little Buttermilk with the French Mocha. Stroke from the tip of the ear into the French Mocha/Soft Black to blend in the highlight color. Wash the brush.

Paint the Highlight Fur and Add Shadows

With Buttermilk and then Titanium White, highlight the fur using the ¼-inch rake brush. Highlight the pup's face on each side of his nose, a little on the cheeks, above the eyes and a little on the temple and forehead. Add highlight fur to the forelegs, the top of the belly and the top of the hind leg. Add more highlight colors if you need to. I thought my pup was too light, so I added more dark fur in this step.

Add tufts of Titanium White fur to the ears using your ¼-inch rake, brushing from the inner edge of each ear toward the outer edge. Load the ¼-inch rake brush with a little thinned Soft Black and add shading to the inner curve of each ear at the edge of the Titanium White hairs. Use only the tips of the bristles and very light pressure. You can also use a no. 1 liner brush for this step.

Float shadows along the bottom of the belly and over the back foot with Soft Black on a 1-inch flat brush. Create a shadow on the bottom edge of the pup and the ground with a back-to-back float of Soft Black. This will help ground the pup, as shown on page 115.

Refer to the sidebar on page 113 for detailed instructions for the eyes.

Painting the Eyes

 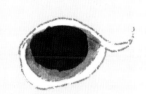

STEP 1: Basecoat the eye with thinned Raw Umber and the pupil with Soft Black.

STEP 2: Shade the upper part of the eye with a sideload float of Soft Black on a no. 8 flat brush. Outline the eye using a no. 0 liner brush loaded with Soft Black.

STEP 3: Highlight the bottom of the eye using the liner brush loaded with Titanium White.

STEP 4: With thinned Mississippi Mud on the liner brush, create the reflection of the sky by painting a thick, wiggly line as shown above. Add the sun highlight with a liner brush and Titanium White at ten o'clock in the left eye and two o'clock in the right eye.

Paint the Black-Eyed Susans

STEP 1: Basecoat the flowers with Tangerine using a no. 6 round brush. Basecoat each petal individually with a stroke pulling from the outside to the center.

STEP 2: Basecoat the stems and leaves with Avocado. Highlight the petals using the no. 6 round loaded with Cadmium Yellow, making a stroke toward the center similar to the basecoating stroke. Allow some of the basecoat to show through. With a small scruffy brush loaded with Raw Umber, pounce in the center of the flowers facing the viewer.

STEP 3: Highlight only the tips of the petals with Yellow Light and Pineapple consecutively. Highlight the stems and leaves with Mint Julep Green using the no. 6 round, and shade with Black Green. Load a no. 0 liner brush with very thin Soft Black, and shade around the base of the petals. Highlight the flower center with thinned Mississippi Mud on the no. 6 round. Finally, outline between the petals and around some petal edges with thinned Raw Sienna on a no. 0 liner.

Finish the Project

Apply two coats of J.W. etc. Right-Step Satin Varnish. Sand lightly with a very fine sanding pad dipped in soapy water. Apply several more coats of varnish, sanding lightly after each.

It's All Small Stuff (White Tiger)

I've always been fascinated by the big cats, especially tigers. There are so few of them in the world today that our children's children may never know of a tiger in the wild. The popularity of white tigers in zoo programs has, unfortunately, led to a lot of inbreeding. There are several wonderful organizations around the world trying to protect these exceptional animals, whether in captivity or in the wild.

Materials List

SUPPLIES:
preparation supplies
   (see page 12)
general supplies
   (see page 13)
finishing supplies
   (see page 13)

BRUSHES:
no. 0, no. 1, no. 2 liners
no. 8 round
¼-inch rake
no. 8, 1-inch flats
1-inch sponge

SURFACE:
fire screen from
   The Tole Booth

DecoArt Americana Acrylic Paints

| Avocado | Jade Green | Reindeer Moss Green | Buttermilk | Titanium White |

| Burnt Umber | Soft Black | Base Flesh | French Mocha | Deep Midnight Blue |

| Blue Mist | Colonial Green | Blue Chiffon | Black Green |

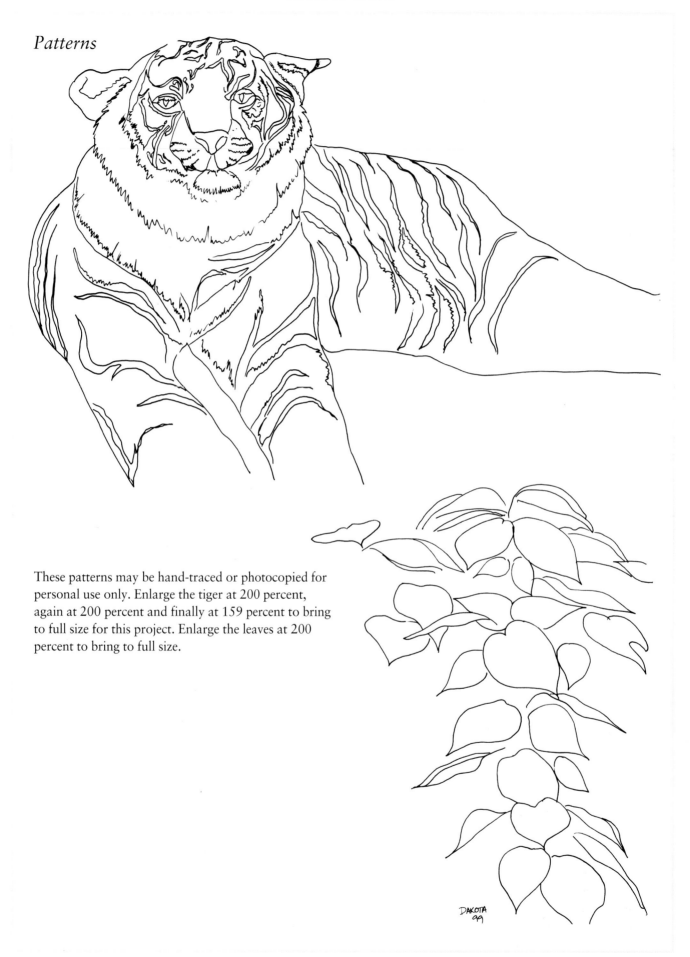

Patterns

These patterns may be hand-traced or photocopied for personal use only. Enlarge the tiger at 200 percent, again at 200 percent and finally at 159 percent to bring to full size for this project. Enlarge the leaves at 200 percent to bring to full size.

Basecoat the Surface

Basecoat the entire fireplace screen with Black Green using a 1-inch sponge brush. You will need to apply at least two coats of the base color. Apply the tiger and leaf patterns with white graphite to the front of the screen.

Paint the Leaves

STEP 1: Basecoat the leaves with Avocado.

STEP 2: Using a ¼-inch rake loaded with Jade Green, brush in the highlights. Reinforce the highlights with Reindeer Moss Green. The light is coming from the upper left.

STEP 3: With the rake brush loaded with Black Green, place shading on the leaves opposite the highlights. Reinforce the highlights further with a little Buttermilk and Titanium White sparingly added in some of the highlight areas.

Shading and Highlighting Placement Guide

Basecoat the Tiger

Basecoat the tiger with Titanium White, following the contour of the tiger with your brushstrokes. Do not worry about completely filling in the tiger; there are many layers to go. Lightly reapply the details of the tiger with black graphite paper and a stylus.

Add the Stripes

With a no. 8 round, paint in the stripes using Burnt Umber, then go over the stripes with Soft Black, especially in the shadow areas. Place stripes near the top of his head with Burnt Umber thinned with a little bit of water. Add the spots from which the whiskers grow with Soft Black. Basecoat the nose with Base Flesh and the nostrils with Burnt Umber.

Shade the Tiger

Shade the tiger with thinned Burnt Umber on a 1-inch flat brush, shading under his chin, on his neck and chest, especially where the forelegs come together. Also shade the right side of his face, the edges of his legs, the top of his head and his belly. Refer to the guide on page 120.

Painting the Eyes

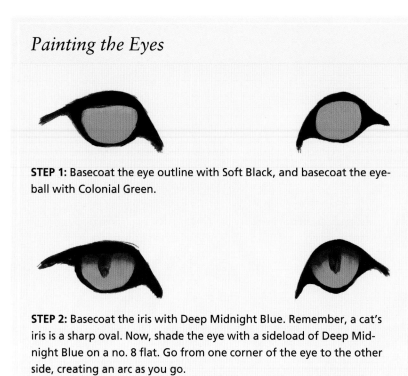

STEP 1: Basecoat the eye outline with Soft Black, and basecoat the eyeball with Colonial Green.

STEP 2: Basecoat the iris with Deep Midnight Blue. Remember, a cat's iris is a sharp oval. Now, shade the eye with a sideload of Deep Midnight Blue on a no. 8 flat. Go from one corner of the eye to the other side, creating an arc as you go.

STEP 3: Add highlights with a no. 0 liner brush loaded with Blue Chiffon. Make a small, thin comma stroke from the edge of the shaded area down toward the bottom of the eye. As you look at the tiger, both the left and right eyes are highlighted on the right side. To add a little reflective light, add a comma stroke of Blue Mist on the other side of the eye from top around to the bottom. Always follow the contour of the eye. Now, add a reflection of the sky in the left eye only. With thinned Blue Mist loaded on the liner brush, dab a line ⅛-inch thick and about ¼-inch long across the eyeball. Don't make it a straight line, there should be slight bumps in it. The right eye doesn't get the sky reflection. Add the sun highlight with a dot of Titanium White on the liner brush at ten o'clock in the left eye and at two o'clock in the right eye.

Add the Fur

Create the fur with the flat of a ¼-inch rake brush loaded with Titanium White. You may need to thin the paint a little with water to make the fur fluffy. Paint most of the fur around the neck, with a little on his face, ears, legs, back and side as it rounds into his back. Make the fur cross some of the stripes so the individual hairs show. Remember to leave some of the shadows showing. The bottom part of the tiger is unfinished because the grass will be painted over this area.

Finish the nose with a sideload of thinned French Mocha on a no. 8 flat brush, and highlights of thinned Buttermilk on a no. 0 liner.

Paint the Grass

STEP 1: Load a 1-inch flat brush with a brush mix of Avocado and Colonial Green, and with the chisel end, make slip-slap, crisscross brushstrokes behind the tiger, in front of him and on each side panel. Apply Avocado in the same manner. These crisscrosses are just to fill in the background grass and shouldn't form a solid sheet of color.

Clean your brush and load with Jade Green. Paint long wavy strokes to make the tall, thin grass. Use the same method to paint a few blades of grass with Reindeer Moss Green. Refine the grass with thinner blades using a no. 2 liner loaded with Jade Green and Reindeer Moss Green consecutively.

⊷ HINT ⊶ *For variety, paint the blades in every direction and vary the lengths and shapes.*

STEP 2: To paint a few grass seeds, load a no. 2 liner brush with the color of the grass blade. At the tip of the blade of grass, make small dots by lightly pressing on the brush. Place a few darker dots at the base of the seed grouping, and lighten the pressure as you progress up until the grass seeds are very small and close together.

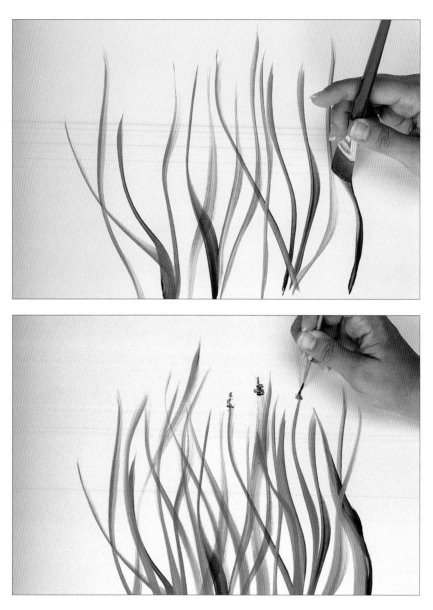

Add the Final Touches

Finally, add the whiskers to the tiger with a no. 0 liner brush loaded with Titanium White thinned to the consistency of ink. The whiskers grow in rows out of the black lines on his nose and hang downward.

To finish the fireplace screen, paint the trim with Reindeer Moss Green and varnish as described on page 13.

125

Organizations:

Society of Decorative Painters
393 N. McLean Blvd.
Witchita, KS 67203
(316) 269-9300
E-mail: sdp@southwind.net
Web site: http://www.nstdp.org

Surface and Materials Suppliers:

Cabin Crafters
1225 W. First St.
Nevada, IA 50201
(515) 382-5406
Fax: (515) 382-3106
Web site: http://www.cabincrafters
.com

Crews Country Pleasures
HCR 64 Box 53
Thayer, MO 65791
(417) 264-7246
Fax: (417) 264-3889

DecoArt
P.O. Box 386
Stanford, KY 40484
(606) 365-3193
Fax: (606) 365-9739
E-mail: paint@decoart.com
Web site: http://www.decoart.com

J.W. etc.
2205 First St., Ste. 103
Simi Valley, CA 93065
(805) 526-5066
Fax: (805) 526-1297
Web site: http://www.jwetc.com

Masterchem
Kilz brand primer
3135 Highway M
Barnhart, MO 63012
(800) 325-3552
Web site: http://masterchem.com
/kilz.html

S & G Products, Inc.
P.O. Box 805
Howell, MI 48844
(517) 546-9240
Fax: (517) 546-9720

The Tole Booth
Heather Redick, CDA
19 Goshen St. N.
Zurich Ontario N0M 2T0
Canada
(519) 236-4945
Fax: (519) 236-7481
E-mail: heather@hay.net
Web site: http://www.decorative
painting.com/heather

Woodcrafts
P.O. Box 78
Bicknell, IN 47512
(812) 735-4829
Fax: (812) 735-3187

Books:

Artist's Photo Reference Birds
by Bart Rulon
North Light Books

Artist's Photo Reference Flowers
by Gary Greene
North Light Books

*Painting the Drama of Wildlife
Step by Step*
by Terry Isaac
North Light Books

*Painting Wildlife Textures
Step by Step*
by Rod Lawrence
North Light Books

To order, call 1-800-289-0963 or write to North Light Books, 1507 Dana Avenue, Cincinnati, OH 45207.

Television Shows:
(check your local listings for dates and times)

BirdWatch
Public Broadcasting System

Kratts' Creatures
Public Broadcasting System

National Geographic Explorer
Public Broadcasting System

Nature
Public Broadcasting System

Wild America
Fox network

Zoos:

Busch Gardens
3605 E. Bougainvillea Ave.
Tampa, FL 33612
(813) 987-5209

Cincinnati Zoo
3400 Vine St.
Cincinnati, OH 45220
(513) 281-4700

Disney's Animal Kingdom
P.O. Box 10000
Lake Buena Vista, FL 32830

San Diego Zoo
Balboa Park
San Diego, CA 92101
(619) 234-3153

Sea World
7007 Seaworld Dr.
Orlando, FL 32821
(407) 363-2200